6-25

Science, technology and the British
industrial 'decline', 1870–1970

New Studies in Economic and Social History

Edited for the Economic History Society by
Michael Sanderson
University of East Anglia, Norwich

This series, specially commissioned by the Economic History Society of Great Britain, provides a guide to the current interpretations of the key themes of economic and social history in which advances have recently been made or in which there has been significant debate.

In recent times economic and social history has been one of the most flourishing areas of historical study. This has mirrored the increasing relevance of the economic and social sciences both in a student's choice of career and in forming a society at large more aware of the importance of these issues in their everyday lives. Moreover specialist interests in business, agricultural and welfare history, for example, have themselves burgeoned and there has been an increased interest in the economic development of the wider world. Stimulating as these scholarly developments have been for the specialist, the rapid advance of the subject and the quantity of new publications make it difficult for the reader to gain an overview of particular topics, let alone the whole field.

New Studies in Economic and Social History is intended for students and their teachers. It is designed to introduce them to fresh topics and to enable them to keep abreast of recent writing and debates. All the books in the series are written by a recognised authority in the subject, and the arguments and issues are set out in a critical but unpartisan fashion. The aim of the series is to survey the current state of scholarship, rather than to provide a set of prepackaged conclusions.

The series has been edited since its inception in 1968 by Professors M. W. Flinn, T. C. Smout and L. A. Clarkson, and is currently edited by Dr Michael Sanderson. From 1968 it was published by Macmillan as *Studies in Economic History*, and after 1974 as *Studies in Economic and Social History*. From 1995 *New Studies in Economic and Social History* is being published on behalf of the Economic History Society by Cambridge University Press. This new series includes some of the titles previously published by Macmillan as well as new titles, and reflects the ongoing development throughout the world of this rich seam of history.

For a full list of titles in print, please see the end of the book.

Science, technology and the British industrial 'decline', 1870–1970

Prepared for the Economic History Society by

David Edgerton
Imperial College, London

CAMBRIDGE
UNIVERSITY PRESS

Published by the Press Syndicate of the University of Cambridge
The Pitt Building, Trumpington Street, Cambridge CB2 1RP
40 West 20th Street, New York, NY 10011–4211, USA
10 Stamford Road, Oakleigh, Melbourne 3166, Australia

First published 1996

Printed in Great Britain at the University Press, Cambridge

A catalogue record for this book is available from the British Library

Library of Congress cataloguing in publication data
Edgerton, David.
  Science, technology, and the British industrial 'decline', 1870–1970 /
prepared for the Economic History Society by David Edgerton.
    p.   cm.
    Includes bibliographical references (p. 73).
    ISBN 0 521 57127 8 (hardback). – ISBN 0 521 57778 0 (pbk.)
    1. Research, Industrial – Great Britain – History – 19th century.
  2. Research, Industrial – Great Britain – History – 20th century.
  3. Technology – Great Britain – History – 19th century.
  4. Technology – Great Britain – History – 20th century.
  I. Economic History Society. II. Title.
  T177.G7E25   1996
  338.94107–dc20   95–50356   CIP

ISBN 0 521 57127 8 hardback
ISBN 0 521 57778 0 paperback

Contents

Tables

Acknowledgements

I am most grateful to the editor of the series for inviting me to write this book. Simon Bellenie helped me to compile an extensive bibliography. Leslie Hannah, Kirsty Hughes, Sally Horrocks, Terence Kealey, John Pickstone and Jonathan Zeitlin have all shaped my thinking on the topics discussed here. Sally Horrocks, Lara Marks, Chris Mitchell, Michael Sanderson, Andrew Warwick and Alan Yoshioka read an early draft and made invaluable criticisms. Alan Yoshioka made penetrating criticisms of a further draft, for which I am very grateful. I am also grateful for additional comments to Paolo Palladino and an anonymous referee. I have also benefitted from the excellent resources of the Science Museum Library.

Note on references

References within square brackets relate to the numbered items in the bibliography. Where given, page numbers are printed in italics, for example [76:*231*]. For ease of reference the bibliography is grouped into related works; within groups the arrangement is roughly chronological.

1
Introduction

The place of science and technology in the British economy, society and government is widely seen as critical to our understanding of the British 'decline'. When other explanations fail – and sometimes before they are examined – clichés such as 'Britain is good at inventing but bad at developing', the 'low status of engineers', the 'two cultures', the 'anti-industrial' and 'anti-scientific' spirit of elites, are trotted out. There is a long tradition of characterising post-1870 Britain by its lack of enthusiasm for science and technology; by the low social status of the practitioners of these obscure mysteries; and by the indifference of government to the needs of technology. More recently supposed deficiencies in research and development (R&D) and patent production have been highlighted.

If we think about the place of science and technology in the world economy we argue very differently. We invoke clichés like the 'ever increasing rates of technological change' or we speak of 'today's technological world', which implies that yesterday's world was not technological. We hear of the 'technological society', the influence of the 'technostructure' and worry about 'technics-out-of-control'. We think of technology as something especially important to the twentieth century, and to the very recent past in particular. There was a time, however, when world and British technological history were much the same thing. Early nineteenth-century Britain was the seat of the Industrial Revolution; it was the workshop of the world; and, it had appropriately heroic entrepreneurs, inventors and engineers. By the end of the nineteenth century, world and British technological history diverge. For the period since the 1870s we have a picture of rapid technological development in the world economy and technological decline in Britain.

Negative pictures of Britain's technology and industry have been painted many times over the past one hundred years. An overall picture is difficult to construct because the case has not been made systematically but all the following elements appear in most versions. Spending on innovation by businesses and by government was low (except after World War II when post-imperial delusions meant a great deal was spent on defence R&D at the expense of civil R&D); this translated into a low rate of innovation. Furthermore, lack of industrial investment, and the lack of trained scientists and (especially) engineers meant that such innovations as there were were not adopted quickly enough; the type of technique in use in British industry was consistently backward. Just as importantly, new industries failed to establish themselves as well as in competitor countries. Such pictures highlight the way in which British performance has deteriorated over time in comparison with other economies. Stress is placed on the falling share of industrial production, manufactured exports, inventions and innovations, accounted for by Britain since the 1870s.

Many reasons have been put forward to explain this poor performance in innovation and in the use of technology. The most popular is that the British elite has been (and in some versions became) hostile to technological education (though less so to scientific education) and as a consequence the output of graduate scientists and engineers was low. In addition, elite institutions such as Parliament, the higher civil service, and the boards of major companies, had low proportions of people trained in science and engineering. This in turn had the consequence that government and business failed to recognise the need to invest in science and technology, compounding the problem.

This book sets out to analyse such arguments in detail, pointing out the different sorts of intellectual traditions they arise in. Indeed one purpose of the book is to pin down arguments which are often presented at such a level of generality that they are difficult to examine and criticise. I hope to show that science and technology play a central, but differing, role in each of a number of different historiographical approaches to the development of the British economy since 1870. The book also goes on to argue that much, perhaps most, of the conventional picture of the role of British science and technology in the industrial 'decline' needs to be reconsidered.

The meaning of 'decline'

Much of the literature on British science and technology since 1870 suffers from a double inversion of historical reality: one of time and one of space. Britain appears to become less technological over time, even though the most obvious feature of British science, technology and industry since 1870 is its expansion, rather than its contraction. British industrial output is much greater today than in 1870; even manufacturing exports are greater. Labour productivity in manufacturing has continued to expand, and manufacturing industry's commitment to innovation has grown even faster than output or productivity. The old chestnut that more scientists were alive in, say, 1960, than in all previous ages put together, applied to British scientists too. The spatial inversion is that other parts of the world are seen as much more technological than Britain, when Britain has been one of the few great technological nations of both the nineteenth *and* the twentieth centuries. Britain not only shared in the great technological developments that have taken place since 1870 but it has been one of the most important sources of such changes. The British economy has been one of the most efficient in the world: of the seven great powers of the interwar years – Germany, France, Italy, Japan, the Soviet Union, the United Kingdom and the USA – only the United States had higher levels of income per head than Britain. From the 1960s, and only since then, all except the Soviet Union overtook Britain although it is important to recognise that the differences between Britain, Germany and France are not very great, and that on some measures Britain is still ahead of Italy and Japan. As we shall see, the strength of British science and technology correlates well with this picture of British economic performance.

We should refocus our historical picture of British technology and change the whole tone of comment and analysis. In order to do this we need to be clear what is meant when historians write of a British economic 'decline'. Economic decline usually means an *absolute* fall or drop in economic activity: by this measure the British economy has only declined for brief periods, for example 1929–32 or 1979–81; usually the economy has grown by a few percentage points each year. By economic decline historians usually mean *relative* economic decline, that is to say a decline in comparison with other economies. The most common comparative measure is rates of growth, and the British economy has indeed *grown* more slowly than the world economy. The consequence – often itself taken as a measure of relative decline – was that Britain's *share* of world production and exports also fell, even as its absolute level of production and exports *increased*.

'Declinist' historians may be distinguished by the fact that they conflate *relative* decline with *doing badly* or *failure*. We should not do this: even if Britain had remained as efficient as the United States throughout the twentieth century it would still have had a lower rate of growth than Germany, Japan or France, and would still have lost share of manufacturing production and exports. The relative decline was thus the product not only of British failings but of other economies improving their previously poor performance. The history of the relative British decline should therefore be the province of the historian of the world economy, as much or more than that of the historian of Britain. As Donald McCloskey has pointed out, much of the literature on the 'decline' of Britain relies on false analogies likening economic development, war and sport. In economic development, unlike war and sport, taking part is indeed enough: everyone can gain, even if not everyone can win. There are now more plausible competitors in the economic race, but everyone now runs faster [18]. Another way of exploring the meaning of relative decline is to explore what a reversal of the decline would entail. If Britain had retained its share of world manufacturing exports of 1950 its exports today would be about three times greater than they actually are. If we assume its production would also be three times greater, today's Britain would be – by a huge margin – the most efficient industrial economy in the world. In short, most, though not all, of the relative decline, as measured in the conventional way, is not due to British failings.

Doubting the use that has been made of the concept of relative decline does not mean rejecting it. When properly understood and used it provides a concise summary of Britain's place in the world economy. What it states is that the British economy was, by comparison with other countries, much more powerful in the past than it is today. This was true of 1870, 1900, 1920 and 1950. Using the concept of the *relative* decline should help shake us out of our present-mindedness when discussing Britain's economic (and scientific and technological) past: it should alert us to the fact that world historical processes have changed Britain's relative position dramatically. As we go back in time Britain produced less and less, but what little it produced carried greater weight in the world. Unfortunately, 'declinist' historians have sought to explain recent relative weakness by finding failure in the past, often as far back as the 1870s. A consistent use of the concept implies that present relative failure should be contrasted with past relative success! It is that past relative success which historians need to describe and explain.

The arguments

The extensive literature on the British economy has long invoked failings in technology as evidence of economic failure, and as a cause of economic failure. The literature on science and technology since 1870 has been strongly influenced by this argument. The inter-penetration of economic history with the history of science and technology, while desirable, has often centred on a particularly 'declinist' version of British economic history and neglected the complexities of the relationship between science, technology and economic performance. In looking at the literature which deals specifically with British science and technology in relation to economic performance we need to be especially attentive to what historians are trying to explain, what assumptions they make, and what explanations they produce. As we shall see, there have been many cases where historians have sought to explain something which was not the case (for example that the German economy was more efficient that the British before the 1960s), or they have assumed relations which do not hold (for example that investment in innovation is the main determinant of rates of growth); and have explained a supposed lack of science and technology using dubious cultural comparisons.

We have no more than sketches of the history of declinist historiography, especially as it relates to science and technology [8][18][21][23][25]. Nevertheless it is clear that while in the late 1950s and 1960s historians tended to lament the poor state of British technology in the past [3][6], by the early 1970s there was a greater emphasis on British technological strength [29] [43][73][74][75]. A surge in condemnations of British technology marked the early 1980s [9][10][13], followed by a new defence of British technology in the early 1990s, for example [16][20]. However, the most striking point to emerge from even a cursory glance at the history of comment on British science, technology and economic performance is that it has been dominated by condemnations the form of which has changed remarkably little over time. One reason for this is that there has been very little debate about the history of British science and technology. Another is that much of the literature simply ignores contrary views and has little sense of its own history.

Given the historical stability of accounts, and the lack of debate between positions, I have chosen to present an analysis of different interpretations, rather than an account of how interpretations have changed over time. The literature on the relations of science, technology and economic performance at world level can be divided into four broad categories: technocratic, neo-Schumpeterian, neo-classical and neo-marxist. While this is not the only categorisation possible, it is especially appropriate here, because it parallels classifications of the debate on the British economic 'decline' [25]. Some words of warning are needed. First, not all authors fall neatly into one category; historians have taken insights from more than one tradition. Second, it is difficult to link these theoretical positions with political positions. Both the left and the right have developed their own versions of technocratic analyses; more broadly, the politics of 'declinism' have changed over time. It is very important, nevertheless, to recognise the political dimensions of the literature [18][21][25].

The single most important tradition of writing on British science and technology in relation to the economy may be labelled *technocratic*, though the term is abhorred by its proponents. It is the account most centrally concerned with the relation between science and technology and economic performance, and is well represented in the extensive science and technology policy literature [9][15][132]. Its most important analytical tool is the degree of scientific and technical expertise to be found in government, business, and social *elites*, and its central claim is that the presence of properly trained elites, and consequent investments in science and technology, determine economic performance. The dominant form of the technocratic argument in Britain has been the *critique* of elites for not being scientific and technical enough; the British elite is pictured as being 'generalist' and 'amateur' and university educated, if at all, in the classics or arts. This technocratic critique was well established by the late nineteenth century and has been revived many times since. Criticism of British technical education, and of the failure of British elites to be technically educated, was particularly strong before and during the Great War [8], in the late 1950s and early 1960s [3][4], and in the 1980s [9][10][13].

An important feature of the technocratic literature is a lack of awareness of continuity in its arguments. There has been a 'disinvention of tradition'. As one historian, writing in the early 1970s, has noted:

Statements made by shipbuilders and engineers over the second half of the nineteenth century give the modern reader a strong sense of *déjà vu*. They were continually aware of the poor quality of apprenticeship programmes and of the need to supplement them with technical education. The *Transactions* of the professional societies contained frequent laments on the existing arrangement and suggestions for improvement, yet the comments have a curiously static quality. For over fifty years each new generation found the same conditions, proposed the same broad remedies, and cited much the same reasons for failure; and each time their remarks were greeted as original and salutary   [44:225].

One reason arguments appeared 'original and salutary' is that writers ignore their antecedents, except to argue that there were a few prescient characters who saw straws in the wind. Where the technocratic critique does see continuity – indeed insists on it – is in the dominance in Britain of an anti-technological culture. So much so, in fact, that much technocratic writing is not economic or technological history but the *cultural* history of anti-technology, as may be seen in the work of C.P. Snow, Martin Wiener and Correlli Barnett [4][10][13]. There is, however, a profound ambiguity in their critiques: they do not differentiate adequately between a pro-technological culture, a pro-industrial culture, and a pro-capitalist culture. They are not the same thing: Barnett, for example, is hostile to free-market capitalism [21].

In recent years historians have responded vigorously to Wiener and Barnett's 'cultural critique'. They argue that British *elite* culture was similar to that in Germany or France or the United States, and that *elite* culture was not as important to economic performance as has been made out [16][17][19][20][23]. Some have gone further and denied that British culture was anti-business or anti-technology. By a neat irony these historians tend to be critical of naive enthusiasm for technology and have sought to explain something which the technocratic tradition argues did not happen: that the British invested, even over-invested, in science and technology [19][20][23][101][106][111][118].

The most fundamental criticism of the technocratic literature is that there is no straightforward link between investment in science and technology, the presence of a proper technocratic elite, and economic growth/efficiency [16][21][28][125][126] [127][130][131][135]. The technocratic literature may also be criticised for failing to address such criticisms. Indeed, it shows little evidence of systematic reviewing of the literature and very little cumulation of knowledge over time. This is ironic given that science and technology are supposed to develop cumulatively, and that the technocratic tradition is so obsessed with what we should learn from the past. Much of the literature is, we may point out with heavy irony, the work of 'amateurs' and 'practical men'.

The neo-Schumpeterian tradition, which reflects the analyses of modern capitalism made by the Austrian economist Joseph Schumpeter, puts *innovation* at the centre of its account of economic development [22]. Closely linked is its emphasis on qualitative rather than quantitative changes in economic and technological history; this is in turn linked to an argument that what may be efficient in the short term may prove inefficient in the long term (the distinction between static and dynamic efficiency). Neo-Schumpeterians argue that in the nineteenth century the key innovator was the heroic, unpredictable *entrepreneur*, but that in the twentieth century he was replaced by the large firm which innovated in a *routinised* way particularly through its

research and development department [6:*326-58*]. A characteristic way of discussing the British economy and British technology
is to argue that the British economy has declined relatively,
especially in that it lost industrial *leadership*: Britain ceased to be
the major site of *innovation* and consequent qualitative changes in
technology. This is then explained by *entrepreneurial* failure in the
late nineteenth century, and a kind of *corporate* failure in the
twentieth [6][12][22][76][79]. One of the key charges against
British businesses is that they failed to develop the in-house
research and development facilities essential to modern, routinised innovation [76]. The main criticisms of the neo-Schumpeterian approach have come from neo-classical economic
historians. They tend to be skeptical of most notions of 'decline',
preferring systematic inter-economy comparisons of efficiency,
which show British performance in a different light [18][26:*62-
89*][27:*95-122, 123-67, 318-46*]. More specifically, they have
argued that most cases of supposed 'entrepreneurial failure' to
adopt new technologies between 1870 and 1914 were in fact
rational responses to economic conditions. More generally, it can
be argued that the neo-Schumpeterian position overemphasises
innovation and the economic significance of new industries, and
over-generalises from US examples. It can be argued that neo-
Schumpeterian analysts have given a quite misleading picture of
British industrial innovation.

The main argument of the neo-classical tradition in economic
history and the history of technology is that economies, and
choices of technique, may be modelled adequately assuming that
businesses act rationally in the face of conditions given by existing
markets [5][18]. Another characteristic is the *quantitative* measurement of the impact of the *diffusion* of particular techniques
[29][31] and of long-run changes in economic efficiency. Some
neo-classical economists have shown a notable skepticism about
the role of innovation in determining *national* economic performance [28][127][130][131] and particularly about the value of
large scale, state-funded technical development [28][106][110]
[111][118]. Others, however, have sought to explain deficiencies
in British total factor productivity, in the interwar and post-Second
World War years, in terms of a lack of appropriate R&D [27:*123-
67*] [121]. The main criticisms of the neo-classical approach

(which come from the technocratic, Schumpeterian and neo-marxist traditions) are that it does not properly deal with innovation or qualitative change, and does not recognise the central role of major institutions like large firms, or the nature of the shopfloor, in shaping economic development.

The neo-marxist tradition of commentary on British science and technology, which dates back to the 1930s, has argued that capitalism has increasingly under-supported innovation, misused it, and misdirected it [7][11]. The British neo-marxist literature has, however, been concerned largely with the state [7]. Some of this literature is concerned with the history of left-leaning scientists and their political role [7][86][90]. While it has criticised the failure of the private sector to fund R&D enough, its main focus has been military R&D funding by the state [2][86]. For the period since 1945 the main emphasis has been on the high British spending on defence R&D which, it is argued, took place at the expense of civil R&D [9:*100–121*][90][96]. In this view the global, commercial and financial orientation of the British state has militated against the development of a national-technocratic modernisation of industry (by, for example, a 'developmental state') which is seen as a key cause of the British decline [25]. The main criticisms are that a national-technocratic policy of modernisation would not have worked, and that the British state has indeed been a 'developmental state' in the military sphere, and to a lesser extent in the civil sphere [20][25]. In addition the literature suffers from a misplaced focus on the left, ignoring the technocratic, modernising traditions of the right [20][91].

A more recent neo-marxist tradition has focussed on the relation of technology and work organisation. In this tradition the nature of the *shopfloor* is just as important as the economic variables of the market in determining technical choice and the efficiency with which technique is used. A characteristic explanation of the British decline is that management failed to gain control of the way work is done [22][26:*90-116*][38]. A similar approach has been used in accounts of the development of academic laboratories in the late nineteenth century which stress their similarities to factories, not just because they used machines, but because they also imposed a highly disciplined labour process on 'scientific workers' [54][55][58].

Evidence and interpretation

We have, then, four traditions of thinking about the relations of science, technology and British economic performance, each with its own focus and explanatory frameworks. Each draws attention to different aspects of the problem, and deploys and develops different kinds of evidence. Nevertheless, they often hold in common a shared picture of the overall structure and performance of British science and technology since 1870. There is a great deal wrong with this standard picture. We need to be very aware of the complex relations between historical actors' accounts and those of historians. Indeed it is vital to treat each separately and to note that historians both sometimes draw too uncritically on actors' accounts, and also fail to put actors' accounts into their proper historical context.

   Much discussion of British science and technology relies uncritically on the testimony of scientists, engineers and industrialists. Undoubtedly they have accentuated negative features as part of campaigns for increased public funding [8][42]. Equally, political debate about British science and technology is not a good source for understanding the state of British science and technology since the political salience of the issue was not directly linked to what was happening [91]. One should tentatively bear in mind that complaints were strongest, paradoxically, in periods of exceptionally rapid growth in funding. Scientists and engineers have also systematically played down the significance of the military in the funding of science and technology [105]. There has also been an over-reliance on government documents, which also downplay the significance of the military, and do not deal in any detail with industrially funded technology [80]. As a result we have an unduly *state-centred* view of British science and technology, focussed on *civil* science and technology, and on *complaints* of lack of funding.

   There are also problems of interpretation, also often deriving from an uncritical use of primary sources. One especially important one is the notably nationalistic treatment of science and technology. The international nature of innovation and diffusion of techniques is much understated [81]. One of the worst problems is the poor quality of international comparisons. Work on technology and relative decline is necessarily comparative, but too often comparisons are not made with a real other country. As Sir John Clapham put it in 1938: 'No doubt an engineer with faith in electric trams for cities, or in milling cutters for all kinds of metal-work, is apt to overdo the backwardness of his countrymen and the deadly universal efficiency of someone else' [1:*155*]. The use of such evidence has been one reason why quite astonishing mis-representations of the comparative development of science and technology abound in the British literature.

Definition is a surprisingly important problem in discussing the history of science and technology. Both 'science' and 'technology' are extremely difficult concepts and practices to define, and we use widely differing implicit definitions. In most European languages the term 'science' covers a wide range of knowledges; by contrast, technology is restricted to the *study of* 'technique' from which it is clearly distinguished. In English 'science' is restricted to natural science, and 'technology' includes machines, structures and pro-cesses. Sometimes, 'technology' is subsumed within 'science' and it is very commonly argued that changes in 'technology' derive from advances in 'science': 'technology' becomes 'applied science'. Equally it is important to be wary of differences between total research and development (R&D), industrial R&D and industry-funded R&D, and between the very concept of R&D, and invention and innovation. It is important to note that definitions change in time, and with different actors. The appended glossary gives some guidance on these complexities.

Science and technology are often wrongly equated with the creation of *novelty* – with *research, invention,* and *innovation.* One especially annoying problem is the identification of 'science and technology' with *academic research.* In fact, most scientists and technologists, even those working in industry, have worked outside R&D; they dealt with long established processes and practices. One way of clarifying the distinction between science and tech-nology on the one hand, and novelty on the other, is to note that invention and innovation are costs, not benefits, to an economy. Inventions and innovations become economically significant only when they are widely used and are therefore no longer novel. There is a great difference in periodisation between an innovation-centred and a use-centred history of science and technology. The association of science and technology with innovation has also helped diffuse the erroneous notion that the rates of growth of economies are determined by investments in innovation. We should not, in short, conflate the history of science and technology, especially in relation to economic performance, with the history of research and innovation.

If historians have overrated scientific and technological novelty, they have perhaps underplayed the novelty of new kinds of scientific and technological institutions appearing for the first time in the late nineteenth century. The research university and the industrial research laboratory were creations of the late nineteenth century; the whole link between innovation and the study of science and technology dates from this period too: even in 1870 institutionalised scientific and technical *innovation* barely existed [24]. But this innovation too took time to diffuse; science and technology were not transformed overnight. We need to be alive to the very great qualitative changes which have taken place in science and technology since 1870. Qualitative change has been very closely linked to quantitative change: changes in the organisation of scientific and technological activity have been accompanied by a huge increase in activity. The number of scientists and engineers has grown astonishingly fast since 1870 (many times faster than the number of politicians, clergymen or doctors); expenditures on science and technology have grown many times faster than GDP.

Finally, we need to distinguish arguments about science and technology at the level of the world economy, and similar arguments about the British case. At each of these levels the interactions are very different because while the world economy was a closed system the British economy was not. If we grant, as we should, that scientific and technical innovation have been one of the key sources of economic change in the world economy, we should not deduce that *British* science and technology had an equivalent effect on the *British* economy. The British economy made use of the larger pool of world science and technology, just as the world economy made use of British science and technology.

This introduction suggests that we should concentrate on particular issues in relation to particular theoretical traditions. In this pamphlet the main themes are the use of technique in British industry; technical and scientific education; the employment of scientists and engineers in industry; research and development in industry; and, the support of research and development by the state. I divide discussion of these themes between specific chapters concerned with Britain, and a final chapter in which these issues are explored in comparative perspective. For each of the topics I show that many historians have severely underestimated British efforts. In terms of particular types of argument the debate between the neo-Schumpeterian and neo-classical positions about the use of technique by British industry is dealt with in chapter 2. This chapter also looks at the related technocratic arguments about technical and scientific education, and the representation of scientists and engineers in the higher reaches of business. Neo-Schumpeterian arguments about innovation in British industry are examined in chapter 3. Chapter 4 takes up technocratic and neo-marxist arguments about the role of the state in funding R&D and looks also at neo-classical analyses of the net effects of government programmes.

Following the unfortunate focus of the literature, I will ignore Ireland, including, after 1922, Northern Ireland, despite the fact that for half the period covered here the whole of Ireland was part of the United Kingdom. The characters in this book are almost exclusively male, reflecting the historical fact that women were a tiny minority in industrial science and technology, as well as the bias of the historiography. A glossary and an annotated bibliography follow the main text.

2

Use of technique and technical and scientific training

From 1870 to the present day there have been constant complaints that Britain has failed to develop new industries, and that its industries have used outdated equipment. Similarly, it has long been argued that old skills persisted and new ones failed to gain a grip. These complaints have been taken up and amplified by historians. As a result the general picture we have of British industry is of technical backwardness. It is little surprise that many historians have sought to *explain* this allegedly poor performance. As we will see, the question of choice of technique has been debated from neo-Schumpeterian, neo-classical and neo-marxist perspectives. By contrast, the closely related question of skill and expertise remains largely the realm of technocratic critiques.

Technique

Over the hundred years 1870–1970 there were dramatic changes in the techniques of production used in British industry. We may cite just a few examples, first of the loss of techniques. In 1870 British shipping still operated many sailing ships but they were rare by 1914; the production of alkali using the Leblanc process was phased out in 1914–18; by the 1960s cotton was no longer spun and woven on the venerable spinning 'mules' and 'Lancashire' looms. The other side of this process of loss was the gaining of new techniques: steel steamships to replace sailing ships; the Solvay and electrolytic processes which came to dominate alkali production; the ring spindles and automatic looms of a modernised cotton industry. Just as important was the installation of equipment to make things that had not been made in 1870: chemical plant to make synthetic dyestuffs and pharmaceuticals; transfer machines to make motor car parts; fractionating columns to refine petroleum; production lines for the assembly of radios and television sets. In short, an inventory of machines in 1970 would be very different from an 1870 inventory. It would also be much larger in terms of value and also probably in sheer physical bulk.

We should not expect product or process innovations to be taken up immediately or even very quickly. Large-scale electricity generation and the motor car were innovated in the 1880s and 1890s, but employment in these industries peaked well after the Second World War; it was only then that electricity and car use became nearly universal, at least in Britain. Nasbeth and Ray have studied the comparative diffusion of industrial processes in many countries and found that techniques innovated in the 1940s, 1950s and early 1960s had by the late 1960s not taken over all production; even in 1981, a follow up study showed, only a few had diffused to near saturation [36][37]. Industrial machines could and did have very long working lives.

Although the yardstick was often unclear, many historians have condemned British industrialists for continuing to use old equipment, and for failing to develop new industries. One explanation was that there was a failure of British *entrepreneurship*: British businessmen, especially between 1870 and 1914, did not innovate, or adopt new technique, with the alacrity of their foreign competitors. One very influential response to this essentially Schumpeterian argument came from neo-classically oriented economic historians. Following Habbakuk's pioneering application of economic thinking to technical choice [5], 'cliometricians' or 'historical economists' from the New World came to the rescue of the dead capitalists of the Old. They re-examined many cases of supposed 'entrepreneurial failure'. They showed in case after case that given the raw materials available, existing market conditions, and costs of labour and capital, British capitalists behaved exactly as capitalists would be expected to: they took on new processes when they were profitable. These studies combined an analysis of the extent of diffusion and of the economic significance of techniques [29][30]. Excellent surveys and summaries are [31] [26:62-89].

However, the claim that there was failure persists. Coleman and MacLeod, for example, drawing on contemporary complaints by industrialists and others, paint a picture of British industrialists as resistant to and ignorant of new technique right into the 1940s [32]. Barnett looked at British industrial performance in the Second World War and found appalling inefficiencies, notably in new industries like aircraft and electronics [13]. Barnett's picture of the aircraft industry has been challenged by comparative analysis [21][39]; similarly, it is not clear what comparative standard Coleman and MacLeod had in mind when they indicted British industrialists [14][18]. Underlying the newer critical picture of British industry is a neo-Schumpeterian critique of the free market and of the neo-classical approach to understanding the economy. While the neo-classical historian Lars Sandberg entitled a review paper on pre-1914 British business, 'The entrepreneur and technological change'[31], neo-Schumpeterian critics have argued that neo-classical analysis did not deal with either. Instead it dealt with rational businessmen responding to *existing* market and technical conditions. The business of the entrepreneur (as opposed to the manager) was to go beyond existing market constraints. This was done through technological and other innovation, but neo-classical analysis had nothing to say on this. In essence, the argument of the neo-Schumpeterians is this: the British economy did behave as a neo-classical economist would expect: it was a highly competitive, and successful, economy before 1914. This was exactly the problem: while Britain had many perfectly rational managers concerned with static efficiency, it had few real entrepreneurs concerned with dynamic efficiency. British industry could not therefore make the qualitative changes in technology, work organisation, and firm structure that were required to increase productivity in the long run. British capitalism remained stuck in an older form of competitive, individualistic capitalism [12] [79]. Such arguments were put forward by Lazonick in influential studies of the cotton textile industry's failure to adopt ring spindles and automatic looms. Lazonick blamed the absolute decline of the industry on the fact that a competitive industry with weaving organisationally separate from spinning could not adopt the new techniques [34]. However, comparative evidence on spinning techniques, and on the uptake of new techniques in the 1940s and

1950s, has cast doubt on this picture [35]. The general argument is, however, that British businesses were too beholden to the market, and did not develop the powerful 'visible hand' of modern corporate capitalism [12][22].

A second development in argumentation considered the relations of technique to the organisation of the workplace. The older literature attacked well-organised British workers for resisting new technique either directly, or by imposing manning levels which made the new technique unviable. The new line of enquiry opened up by neo-marxist historians suggests that managers in Britain, in contrast to the United States, never even sought to achieve complete control of the workplace. Workers had a considerable amount of discretion over the intensity and organisation of work. The other side of this coin was the underdevelopment of management, and the consequent failure to get the necessary returns from high-throughput, capital-intensive technique. In short, British industry did not come to emulate the style of mass production pioneered by the Ford Motor Company in the USA, even though it had 'Fordist' technology available to it [26:*90–116*][33][38]. Zeitlin has put forward a new interpretation, suggesting that British industry achieved a great deal of success with flexible craft production, but was seduced by the apparently greater claims of Fordist mass production [39].

Expertise

Just as the techniques of production in British industry changed so did the skills and expertise of workers and managers: skills and knowledges disappeared, and new skills and knowledges were created and diffused. Particularly startling has been the increase in employment in industry of people with higher education. Hardly any graduates were employed in industry in 1870; by 1970 they represented a small but very significant proportion of the workforce. Historians have long insisted that this process happened far too slowly in Britain, and have linked this to the allegedly poor record of British industry in modernising old industries and creating new ones.

Interestingly enough, very little of this literature is concerned with experts actually working in industry; it deals predominantly with higher scientific and technical *education*, and the place of science and technology in elite culture. In the late 1950s C.P. Snow and Donald Cardwell argued that British culture, and higher education particularly, undervalued technical education [3][4]. Similar arguments were powerfully expressed by Landes [6:*343–7*]. A particularly important aspect of these arguments is the idea of 'two cultures'. This was most clearly put forward by C.P. Snow, but variants run right through discussions of British technical education. It involves not just a dichotomy between 'science' and 'literature', but between North and South, aristocracy and middle class, finance and industry. The 'two cultures' were not equivalent: the traditional literary culture, it is argued, dominated the British metropolitan, aristocratic elite; science was a socially subordinated culture, associated with the provincial middle class [4]. Science is red-brick, not Oxbridge; it is Manchester not London; it is Harold Wilson and not Harold Macmillan; it is, furthermore, politically radical rather than conservative. Within this scheme, technology is further subordinated under science, suggesting the particular weakness of British engineering.

The picture of a dismally backward technical education was challenged by Sanderson in 1972, in what remains the best general treatment of British higher scientific and technical education [43]. Nevertheless, in the late 1970s and early 1980s historians who either dismissed or ignored the debates of the economic historians on the quality of British business restated the conventional thesis [12][47]. Martin Wiener and Correlli Barnett argued forcefully for the poor development of technical education, and put this at the centre of their arguments about the British decline. Both made the case that British higher education turned its back on science, and especially engineering. Technical education was carried on in low grade institutions, and British industry relied for too long on low-status 'practical men', using notoriously backward 'rule of thumb' methods [10][13]. Both had a point: education at both school and university level was dominated by classics and mathematics. This is not surprising given the very long history of dominance of these subjects. They were wrong about the trends: within the huge expansion of higher education between 1870 and 1914 there was a relative decline of classics and mathematics. Science, engineering,

Table 2.1   *Estimates of annual graduation in science, mathematics and technology. England*

	1870	1880	1890	1900	1910	1914
Cambridge Tripos Part I						
Mathematics	–	–	–	82	–	112
Natural Sciences	–	–	–	136	–	152
Mechanical Sciences	–	–	–	18	–	43
Oxford						
Mathematics	–	–	–	26	–	16
Natural Sciences	–	–	–	37	–	87
Oxford and Cambridge						
(total)	–	–	–	299	–	410
Other English**	19	55	166	378	1,231	–

Sources: G. W. Roderick and M. Stephens, 'Scientific Studies at Oxford and Cambridge, 1850-1914', *British Journal of Educational Studies* 24 (1976), p. 61; G. W. Roderick and M. Stephens, 'Scientific Studies and Scientific Manpower in the English Civic Universities, 1870-1914', *Science Studies* 4 (1974). The figures given for Oxford and Cambridge differ between these two articles.

**The 'Other English' category includes graduates of the Royal School of Mines, the Royal College of Science, and the C&G Central Technical College (together as Imperial College from 1907).

NB: Only a fraction of students attending took degrees, with the exception of Oxford and Cambridge. Many students taking natural sciences in both Oxford and Cambridge went on to medical degrees.

and other modern subjects like modern languages, history and economics developed especially rapidly.

What needs to be explained is not the decline or even the non-emergence of technical education but its rapid expansion [16]. To look at 1870, as for example Gowing has done, is misleading since then there was indeed little going on [47]. Only twenty years later, and especially forty years later, the picture was quite transformed, as may be seen in Table 2.1. The cumulative total graduation from *English* higher education institutions in science and technology, *excluding* Oxford and Cambridge, was 14,330 by 1910 [45]. By then most major English cities had substantial universities of their own (the 'red-bricks' or 'civics') while smaller cities had university colleges. The University of London, in by far the largest city in Britain, included two large university colleges, University College and King's College, and the specialist Imperial College of Science and Technology (1907). Sanderson has pointed out that the civics were the creations of businessmen of the great industrial cities; they were committed to an industrially relevant education and were the embodiment of the industrial spirit in education that Wiener claims was missing [50].

Scientific and technical education was not confined to the new universities. The (by the standards of the civics, very large) ancient English and Scottish universities, especially Cambridge, Edinburgh and Glasgow, were especially strong in engineering. In 1903 there were 226 engineering undergraduates in Cambridge, more than 8% of the student body, making it the largest engineering school in the country [43:45]. Nor was Cambridge physics unconnected to practical concerns [58]. Indeed the rise of laboratory teaching and research in physics was closely linked to industrial concerns [51][54][58]. Contrary to Barnett's claim that there was no integration of liberal and practical instruction in the same institution, in Britain engineering was integrated into the multi-faculty university, even into the ancient universities [21][52].

Another line of criticism of the Wiener/Barnett arguments has looked at the relevance of education to industrial performance before 1914. Since higher *education* only affected a tiny minority of people, even a small minority of businessmen, its impact would have been small [23]. Inter-economy comparisons also suggest that differences in performance are not explained by levels of technical *education* [16][125][126]. To take an example close to home: in 1914 there were 2 students of science and engineering for every 10,000 Scottish residents; for England and Wales the figure was 1 per 10,000 residents [49]. Part of the difference is accounted for by the fact that Scottish degrees were and are longer; nevertheless Scotland was more committed to higher education than England. However, the English economy performed better than the Scottish economy in the twentieth century, not least in the new industries. The point is, as we will note again below, that we should not conflate skill and expertise with *education*, especially before 1914.

Table 2.2 *University students by faculty, 1929–68. Great Britain*

	1929/30 %	1938/9 %	1950/1 %	1967/8 %
Arts and social studies	44.8	38.7	37.2	35.3
Science	17.1	15.2	21.1	28.1
Technology	12.5	13.6	15.8	23.8
Medicine	23.3	30.3	21.0	10.5
Agriculture	2.2	2.3	4.9	2.3
Total	100.0	100.0	100.0	100.0
Female students (FT)	28.3	23.3	22.8	27.4
Part-time and occ.	23.3	21.2	13.7	8.2
	No.	No.	No.	No.
Male students (FT)	32,682	38,368	65,831	144,956
Total male	43,561	49,202	79,422	159,354
Total female	15,913	14,218	22,590	58,275
Grand Total	59,474	63,420	102,012	217,629

Source: adapted from A.H. Halsey (ed.), *Trends in British Society since 1900* (London, 1972), Tables 7.8, 7.13, 7.14.

NB: Note the dramatic fall in part-time and occasional students, caused largely by the increased availability of grants for full-time study. Note also the *fall* in the proportion of full-time students who were female, especially to the 1950s.

Technical and scientific education after 1918

Most of the criticisms of British higher education cover the years before 1914; much less attention has been given to later develop-ments even though we would expect the significance of technical education to have increased. The number of scientists and engineers graduating from British universities was growing after 1918, though not at the rate of the Edwardian years, as is shown in Table 2.2. At the turn of the century some 450 engineering graduates (or equivalent) were being produced by universities and university colleges; by the 1930s some 900 engineers were being turned out [53:*71–2*]. Through the interwar years Cambridge had around 500 undergraduate engineers, about 10% of the undergraduate population. Science training expanded also, and indeed from the Great War the government gave grants for postgraduate research in science and engineering (only). From 1921 a national qualification of near-degree level was available to students in the expanding municipal technical colleges. By the 1930s this route provided about 1,000 engineers a year, about the same as universities [53].

This second layer of higher education was overwhelmingly part-time (and concentrated on evening classes) and therefore linked directly to work. It was also restricted to technological subjects. Barnett, and other critics, do have a point when they insist that such education was educationally and socially second class [13]. The point is not that technical education was second class, rather it should be that second class education was technical education. The highest technical education took place in the universities, alongside science, the humanities, law and medicine. There were two different systems of higher technological education: one catered for those rich enough to afford to study for three years full-time: the other for those who had to work from an early age.

After the Second World War higher education, in both universities and technical colleges, expanded very rapidly indeed. While the older literature makes plain that expansion was driven by the desire to increase the number of science and engineering graduates [40][41][42][43], more recently historians have taken a different view, summarised by Millward [27:*144–50*]. Aldcroft, for example, has argued that 'the main thrust of university expansion was centred on satisfying the demand for arts and social science courses to the detriment of technological and vocationally-oriented subjects' [57:*124*]. This is clearly misleading: compared with the interwar university the postwar university was increasingly oriented towards science and technology (see Table 2.2). One consequence was that by the early 1970s entry into professional engineering was nearly exclusively graduate [9:*81*]. A more appropriate criticism is that British universities paid more attention to science than to engineering. By comparison with other countries, as we will see in chapter 5, this was the case, but the number of engineers graduating in Britain was high. We need to note one especially interesting criticism: that the supply of scientists and engineers was

Table 2.3 *Career destinations of Oxford male science graduates, 1900–70. Percentages*

	1900–13	1920–9	1930–9	1946–52	1960–70
Industry and commerce	15.99	16.68	19.10	27.86	41.76
of which industry	8.00	12.00	10.91	21.75	22.63
Government (including colonial and local)	14.66	10.66	10.01	7.17	9.26
Teaching (school and university)	39.10	34.00	32.73	29.71	26.34
Medicine (largely) and similar	28.44	35.33	34.55	29.71	19.96

Source: Daniel Greenstein, 'The Junior Members, 1900–1990: a profile' in B. Harrison (ed.), *The History of the University of Oxford* Vol. VIII *The twentieth century* (Oxford, 1994), Table 3.5.

over-expanded in the 1950s and 1960s under pressure from the 'science lobby' [42]. This claim, which runs quite counter to the substance and tone of most commentary, deserves serious consideration.

Another recurring complaint was that university education, even in science and engineering, was removed from the needs of industry, and inculcated an anti-industry spirit. These criticisms are difficult to assess, but research suggests that employers had a strong influence on, or were satisfied with, university curricula for engineers [53]. It seems likely that a majority of chemistry students in civic universities were destined for industry, even before 1914 [68][69]. It is also becoming clearer that there was a very active interaction between university departments of science and engineering and industry before 1914, not only in teaching but in research [43][46][48][51][54][55][56][58]. Trends are also significant: from the 1880s onwards increasing proportions of university graduates, in all disciplines, went on to industrial careers [43]. The trend *towards* industry is strikingly clear in the case of Oxford science graduates, shown in Table 2.3.

The expert in industry

There have been many complaints about the low number, and low status, power and authority of technical experts in British industry. Much of the literature implies that British scientists and engineers never ran a British company, that they were poorly trained and socially inferior. Solid evidence on these points is, however, hard to find: our historical picture of scientists and engineers working in industry is very sketchy indeed.

For the earlier part of our period especially, formal higher education captures only a tiny fraction of the process of acquiring higher technical and scientific expertise. Industry undertook its own training. To become a professional engineer in the late nineteenth century required parents to pay an established engineer a substantial fee to take on a boy as a 'pupil' or 'premium apprentice'. These apprenticeships were quite different from the ordinary 'trade' apprenticeships, which were designed to train skilled workers. Even men with degrees in engineering had to undergo a period of (often paid) apprenticeship [53]. There was much to be said for the 'practical man' who would use the time-honoured 'rule of thumb'. Tweedale, notably, has pointed out its continuing significance in metallurgy, and its centrality in making Sheffield the world centre of production of new alloy steels in the beginning of this century [66], though the importance of the work of Professor Arnold of Sheffield University has also been emphasised [48]. Robertson has pointed out that the British shipbuilding industry was the largest, the most efficient, and the most technically advanced in the world despite the poor provision for technical education [44]. Only at the beginning of this century did the engineering institutions (the professional bodies for engineers, for example the Institution of Mechanical Engineers) set examinations for prospective members to pass, and grant exceptions to those who had studied in higher education [53].

Recent research suggests that historians have seriously underestimated the number of formally-qualified scientists and engineers working in British industry. Divall has noted that a significant proportion of members of the Institution of Civil Engineers (which was not restricted to civil engineers in the modern sense) were graduates by 1914, though the situation was very different for mechanical and electrical engineers [53]. Second to engineering the major industrial specialism was chemistry. In this case it is now very clear that many more qualified chemists were employed than has been believed. The widely cited estimate of between 180 and 225 graduate chemists working in industry in 1902 has been questioned [14:*103*][68], and more recent research suggests at least that number engaged in research and development alone [80]. Donnelly was able to identify graduates in industry from a sample taken from those graduating in three-year periods around 1880 and 1900 from five institutions. He found 103 such students who had specialised in chemistry alone. Between 1884 and 1901 no fewer that 71 *Honours* graduates in chemistry entered industry from Owens College, Manchester [68]. If much larger than previously thought, the employment of graduates in industry before 1914 was much lower than levels reached later. The membership of engineering institutions increased from around 4,000 in 1870 to about 40,000 in 1914 and to more than 145,000 by 1957. By the 1920s ICI alone employed about one thousand chemists. By 1964 there were 76,060 qualified scientists and engineers working in manufacturing industry alone [62:*196*].

It has long been suggested that scientists and engineers were very poorly represented in the leadership of British industry. But by mid-century some 20% of the most senior men in British manufacturing had university level scientific or technical education. One study of the boards of publicly quoted engineering companies in 1952 suggested that 21.5% of directors had technical qualifications (16% were chartered engineers); accountants accounted for only 9.5% [59]. Erickson's well-known study of the heads of steel firms, if interpreted correctly, gives similar results [60]. In Table 2.4 I give the results of her analysis as presented, together with a correction to take account of the fact that educational information was only available for a proportion of her sample. These figures also suggest the important role of Oxford and Cambridge in technical education: if we assume that graduates of other universities and colleges all received a technical education, then at least 6% of the 1935-47 sample probably received their technical education in Oxford or Cambridge. That is, about half the technically educated leaders of steel firms had been to Oxford

Table 2.4 *Higher education of active partners or executive directors of steel firms, 1875–1947*

	1875–95	1905–25	1935–47
Oxford or Cambridge			
(a)	9	15	21
(b)	18	26	36
Other university or college			
(a)	6	4	10
(b)	12	7	17
Formal technical training			
(a)	7	9	16
(b)	14	16	28
Apprenticeship*			
(a)	17	12	6
Members of Engineering			
Institutions**	27	26	16

(a) as proportion of total sample, including the large number for whom there was no educational information.
(b) as proportion of sample for which there was educational information.
*This figure is for apprenticeship with or without formal technical education.
**These are actual members as a percentage of total: all members were identified. The fall may well be due to the fact that the institutions became less prone to giving effectively honorary membership to major industrialists.

It is important to note that the sample was not the management grades of the steel firms, but the one or two leaders of each firm. These figures give us no information as to the overall technical resources of the steel firms, and should not be interpreted as such.
Source: Charlotte Erickson *British Industrialists, Steel and Hosiery 1850–1950* (Cambridge, 1959), Chapter 2, Chapter 3 and Appendix G.

or Cambridge. Such a conclusion casts doubt on Coleman's impressionistic picture of the business elite [63]. Coleman argues that the direction of large British firms was, until the 1960s, in the hands of 'gentlemen'. 'Gentlemen' were 'amateurs' who had been through public school, and possibly university (usually Oxford or Cambridge), but had very limited knowledge of applied science and technology. Beneath them were the 'players', socially inferior 'practical men' who were mere technicians unschooled in theoretical science. This dichotomy, which echoes the 'two cultures' argument, is just too neat. There was more scientific and technical expertise (often acquired in Oxford or Cambridge) at board level than the picture implies; similarly, there were more university trained scientists and engineers below board level than the contrast between university-trained 'amateurs' and 'practical men' allows [14]. Equally, we should not assume that all the 'practical men' were players; there were gentlemen trained as engineers by apprenticeship, at least in the aircraft industry [20].

It is also important to be aware of changes in time in the power and authority of scientists and engineers. We have evidence from the histories of ICI and Courtaulds that scientists did rise far in the industrial hierarchy in the postwar years [14]. One study suggests that scientists and engineers dominated at least one of ICI's divisions [71]. In 1952 the nationalised industries had a high proportion of scientists and engineers on their boards: 26.5% were chartered engineers and 36% had formal technical qualifications [59], a picture confirmed by historical studies of electricity supply and the nuclear industry [64][85]. In the case of aircraft too, engineers were very well represented: within British Aerospace they dominated divisional boards [20]. There is some suggestion, however, that from the late 1960s the position of scientists and engineers in the private sector weakened, perhaps because engineer-dominated companies pursued technical excellence without much reference to the market [14][64]. Some international comparisons, unfavourable to British industry, are reported in [9:*88-99*] but see also [139].

3
Industrial invention, innovation, and research and development

One could draw up an impressive list of British inventions and innovations since 1870. It would serve a useful purpose in high-lighting the technical creativity of British industry since 1870. Since 1945, at least, Britain has received more in licences and royalties for technology than it has paid out: it has been a net exporter of technology [15]. This does not mean that the majority of technique in use in Britain was of British origin. It is likely that only a small proportion of the things made in Britain, let alone consumed in Britain, could be traced back to British inventors and innovators. Assuming that Britain used all the significant innovations available in the world then the proportion of foreign techniques used in Britain will be the same as the proportion of world innovations that are non-British. We have some very crude figures (Table 5.15) which would suggest that between 1876 and 1900 only 14% of technique was of British origin. The assumption of free trade in technique may, however, be quite misleading for a large part of the twentieth century; there was a degree of technological autarky, especially from the 1930s to the 1960s. Certainly, some technical developments took place in Britain only because there were tariff and other import barriers [107][117].

British industry did acquire much important technique first used elsewhere. Classic examples are machinery for making small arms imported from the USA in the 1850s; the Solvay process for alkali, first developed in Belgium; and from Germany, the contact process for sulphuric acid, the Haber–Bosch process for synthetic ammonia, and the internal combustion engine. Similarly foreign industries acquired British-innovated techniques: examples are the Bessemer converter, the spinning mule, and viscose rayon. A still notorious case was the British innovation of synthetic dyestuffs, which was taken up by the German chemical industry. The failure of British firms to develop and produce synthetic dyestuffs for the giant British textile industry has long been condemned, despite the fact that the total value of such dyestuffs was small [1][16].

British innovation has attracted a great deal of attention from historians concerned with British economic performance. The loss of innovative leadership has been held to be responsible for some of the 'decline' of British industry. This is particularly the case in the Schumpeterian tradition, where innovative success is sometimes made to appear the same thing as economic success. Similarly, in the technocratic tradition we often find the assumption that innovation and economic success go together. While some historians hold that British industry has been consistently bad at innovating [15][76], others argue that Britain, and British industry, has been good at innovating, especially after 1945, but bad at exploiting these innovations [75].

There is no doubt that there has been a relative decline in British innovativeness: in 1970 Britain accounted for a much smaller share of world innovations than it did in 1870. Of course, such a relative decline in innovation is fully consistent with an absolute increase in innovation and since 1870 there has been a huge increase in the resources devoted to innovation in Britain. Unfortunately, we only have very partial measures of innovation so it is difficult to chart this growth and relative decline. The first measure is patents, that is new inventions registered for the grant of a temporary monopoly. However, not all technical advances are patented, and most patents turn out to be economically useless. The second is innovations, that is the first application of inventions, patented or not. These can be found in a variety of ways, from combing books of economic history, to – for more recent periods – asking technical experts what significant innovations they have come across. Such lists have the great disadvantage that one cannot legitimately draw conclusions about change over time. The third measure, that of R&D expenditure, can only be used for the period since the 1930s, though estimates have been made for the earlier period.

The relations between these measures are complex and change over time. A survey of more than 4,000 British innovations made

Table 3.1 *Queen's Awards for Innovation in 1966 and 1967 by industrial sector*

	Number of innovations	% innovations	% of total qualified R&D staff, 1965
Food, drink and tobacco	1	1.2	2.4
Chemical and allied	7	8.3	15.4
Metal manufacture	1	1.2	4.1
Electrical engineering	3	3.6	6.5
Mechanical engineering	25	29.8	9.6
Electronics	16	19.0	13.2
Motor and other vehicles	5	6.0	1.9
Aircraft	7	8.3	7.8
Textile, clothing etc.	2	2.4	2.8
Other manufacturing	10	11.9	5.2
Total manufacturing	77	91.7	68.9
Construction	3	3.6	0.6
Research associations	2	2.4	3.7
Nationalised industries	1	1.2	4.5
Central government	0	0.0	16.1
Atomic Energy Authority	1	1.2	5.9
Local authorities	0	0.0	0.4
Total non-manufacturing	7	8.4	31.2
Grand Total	84	100.0	100.0 (53,900)

Source: John Langrish *et al.*, *Wealth from knowledge* (London, 1972), p. 64.

between 1945 and 1983 (found by asking technical experts) shows that innovations follow the distribution of patents across industrial sectors and across firm size. However, neither corresponded well to the distribution of R&D spending: innovation and invention were less concentrated by sector and firm than R&D [77]. We can see the same effects in Table 3.1. This suggests very strongly that R&D is not the only source of innovation, even in R&D-performing firms. For the years before 1945 we might expect an even less close connection between patents/innovations and R&D. There are two reasons for believing this. First, the long-term trends in patenting and R&D have been quite different: over the twentieth century patenting has grown less fast than GDP, while R&D has grown much faster [82]. Secondly, well into the twentieth century, individuals were a more important source of patents than corporations but by definition R&D cannot be done by individuals. We must not be too tempted, therefore, by the thesis that at the end of the nineteenth century the character of invention and innovation changed dramatically: that the single inventor gave way to the corporate, routinised invention of the new 'science-based' industries with research and development laboratories [6:*423–6*]. Even in 1914 industrial laboratories were rare, but innovation was proceeding strongly. The development of great new ships, motor cars and aviation are, rightly, not associated with laboratories, but should not be ignored for that reason [83]. We should also remember that a minority of scientists and engineers, even of those employed in manufacturing industry, were engaged in R&D [69][70][78:*106–34*].

Research and development

We know much more about research and development in British industry than about invention or innovation. Around 1870 organised research and development was practically unknown, but by the Edwardian years expenditure was running at perhaps £500,000 per annum. We know of more than 20 British firms doing R&D before 1914 [73][80]. The Great War had an important impact on industrial research. In many firms research activity greatly expanded, and started in others. This is surprising since an emergency like war would not be expected to stimulate a long-range activity like R&D. However, the breakdown of international trade, and the demand from the armed services for new equipment, played a key role. By the 1920s industry's R&D spending was probably above £2m. There was a small cut in expenditure in the early 1930s, but by 1938 it was at least £5.4m (see Table 3.2). By the end of the interwar years industrial research was a well-known feature of British industry [80].

By 1945, perhaps 50% more qualified scientists and engineers were employed in industrial R&D than in 1938. Expenditure increased a great deal more, to perhaps twice prewar levels in

Table 3.2 *Estimates of industry-funded research and development spending. UK £m.*

	1 FBI estimates	2 Industry-funded	3 Industry-funded 1980 prices
1930	2.170	–	*36
1935	3.370	–	*56
1938	5.442	–	*90
1941	6.120	–	–
1945	21.815	10.000	–
1950	23.779	23.779	200.0
1955		77.300	505.2
1958		160.200	905.1
1961		277.700	1461.6
1964		313.600	1522.3
1966		392.900	1761.9
1967		410.200	1971.3
1968		427.000	1801.7
1969		444.800	1815.5
1972		507.200	1570.3

*Very crude estimates assuming 1930s prices are half 1950 prices.
Sources: (1) D.E.H. Edgerton and S.M. Horrocks. 'British Industrial Research and Development before 1945', *Economic History Review* 47 (1994), p. 219, Table 2 and Table 4. Note that with the exception of the figure for 1945 these figures exclude aircraft. Since aircraft R&D was largely state funded, aircraft R&D was subtracted from the 1945 figure, with a small allowance for other military-funded R&D, to give the crude estimate of 10m for privately funded R&D for 1945 given in column 2. (2) and (3) David Edgerton, 'British Research and Development after 1945: a re-interpretation', *Science and Technology Policy* (April 1993).

constant prices. It is almost certain that most of this expansion came from increased state expenditure in industry. Indeed after the war there were periods when government funding of R&D in industry exceeded industry's own funding. In the late 1960s government funding still accounted for around 30% of R&D done in industry. Most of this government funding was for defence, and will be considered in the following chapter. However, after 1945 industry-funded R&D itself grew at a spectacular pace, indeed at many times the rate of growth of manufacturing output. Between 1950 and 1961 private funding increased sevenfold (see Table 3.2), a much greater rate of increase than in the interwar years. Only in the late 1960s did expenditure fall, both in absolute terms, and as a proportion of manufacturing output.

R&D spending has been highly concentrated in manufacturing industry: very little was done in the service industries, utilities or construction (see Table 3.1). In the case of electricity, for example, electrical manufacturing firms, rather than generators and distributors, have dominated R&D. Within manufacturing, R&D expenditures have been concentrated in a few sectors, notably the chemical, electrical and aircraft industries. The sectoral distribution of R&D spending within manufacturing has shifted, especially due to the rise in spending on R&D in pharmaceuticals: firms in this industry were only middling R&D spenders in the 1930s, but by the 1970s they were among the largest spenders [135]. R&D was not confined to chemicals, electricals and pharmaceuticals; it was also important in steel, in textiles, in engineering; indeed R&D has been a feature of all manufacturing sectors. It is especially important to note the very high concentration of R&D in a few large manufacturing firms.

The debate about industrial R&D

There has been a tendency to underestimate the amount of R&D supported by British firms which has passed into the historical literature. Before the first estimates of industry-funded R&D were published in 1943 information was scarce, but reasonable guesses could be made [80]. By the 1970s however, the impression had been gained that the research efforts of British firms before 1939 had been feeble, and that government-funded civil research was more important. More recently, David Mowery has argued that, in contrast to the US firms, British firms had underdeveloped in-house laboratories, and relied instead on partly government-funded cooperative research associations [76]. Mowery's argument has proved influential despite the fact that Sanderson had shown in 1972 that industrial R&D spending was much higher than the spending of the research associations [73]. Certainly, the industrial research association was a peculiarly British phenomenon, but it was not typical of industrial R&D as a whole. Research association spending was only about 10% of industry's in-house spending [80].

Historians writing in the 1970s gave a generally upbeat account of interwar in-house industrial R&D [73][74][75]. North American historians writing in the 1980s have given a very different picture, insisting that British industry did not develop the large, research-intensive firms that characterised US industry. Mowery complained that only 20 of Britain's largest 200 companies undertook research in the 1930s [76]. Mowery not only argued that British industry did not do enough R&D. He also argued that R&D was done inefficiently and that resulting innovations were ineffectively used. Nonetheless, apart from the fact that the British economy allegedly performed badly, there is no direct evidence to support Mowery's assertions [76]. Chandler noted that 'the few firms that did make important investments in research, such as ICI, Burroughs Wellcome, and Dunlop, did begin to develop a broader line of products. They remained the exceptions, however' [79:390]. Edgerton and Horrocks have argued against this picture, noting that by the 1930s most large British manufacturing firms were doing R&D and that this R&D was highly concentrated in the largest firms [80].

Mowery's explanation for poor R&D performance was that British industry had a deficient structure: it did not measure up to the standards of the large US corporation as described in the work of Alfred Chandler [80]. Secondly, he argued that British higher scientific and technical education was deficient, but his account was rather different from the one given above; indeed Mowery, by a misreading of the figures, mistakenly believed that there were only 24,000 students in British universities in the mid-1920s. There were in fact at least twice that number (see Table 2.2). Thirdly, he argued that the government, instead of encouraging the development of in-house R&D, helped create ineffectual research associations. He neglected the fact that the main purpose of research associations was to help those firms too small to support R&D themselves; the government believed large firms could and did support R&D [80]. In any case the government's major spending on industrial R&D was through the service ministries and not through research associations (see chapter 4 below). There has been less debate among historians about industrial R&D after 1945. This is perhaps due to the fact that attention has been concentrated on government-funded programmes for military and civil aircraft, and nuclear technology. We know much less about the R&D programmes of private firms, even though some economists and historians have drawn attention to their importance [72][75]. We can, however, discern three broad views about such programmes. Saul has argued that British industry was highly innovative between 1945 and 1965, but the problem was that 'British firms, for the most part, did not possess the resources or the flair to exploit what had been discovered' [75:*123*]. The second view, which was present from the late 1950s, was that British firms were in general too small to support the large R&D budgets required to carry out R&D effectively. The comparison was made almost exclusively with US industry. The Labour government of 1964–70's Industrial Reorganisation Corporation took up this argument and many of Britain's largest R&D spending firms were merged with government support. Remarkably, the late 1960s merger boom coincided with an absolute fall in industrial R&D spending, and indeed a fall in the R&D/output ratio for manufacturing industry [135]. This fall in industrial R&D was much commented on from the mid-1970s [133:*92–6*].

The third, and most popular, view derives from comparative studies. The 1960s saw the creation of internationally standardised comparative data on R&D through the work of the OECD, and the development of academic units dealing with science policy. Comparative and policy-oriented studies have argued that by comparison with Germany and Japan, R&D spending in British industry was heavily weighted towards government-funded defence and 'prestige' projects. The reader is left to infer that British industry was doing less 'bread-and-butter' R&D than Japanese or German industry at least in the late 1950s and 1960s. Anticipating the detailed discussion in chapter 5, we may state that before the mid-1960s British industry spent more of its own money on R&D, in both absolute and relative terms, than the industries of Japan, Germany, France and Italy, and indeed any capitalist country other than the United States [135].

4
State funding of research and development

Unlike nineteenth century Continental European states, the British state did not involve itself directly in most areas of technological development, at least within the United Kingdom: the Empire was another matter [88]. There was, however, one great exception to this rule: the armed services. They not only trained technical personnel, but also engaged in the development and production of weapons of war. Although from the early twentieth century the state increased its involvement in the funding of research and development for civil purposes, it was not until the late 1960s that the state spent more on civil R&D than on warlike R&D. The state came to monopolise the funding of military R&D, by contrast, industry always funded more civil industrial R&D than did the state (see Tables 4.1 and 4.2).

Despite this pattern of expenditure, the extensive literature on science and the British state concerns itself, without adequate warning, with state funding of R&D for *civil* purposes [105]. Indeed it concentrates on the Department of Scientific and Industrial Research (DSIR), the only government department with science or research in its title. Historians have paid much less attention, not only to the military, but also to the significant units dealing with medical research, the Ministry of Agriculture and Fisheries, the Post Office and the BBC. Even the service and supply departments were larger funders of *civil* R&D than the DSIR (see Table 4.2) [103][104]. Despite the protests of scientists, and the laments of historians of 'science policy', the British state usually spent more on warlike R&D than on civil R&D, and never concentrated its funding of R&D in one department of state [84][87].

Table 4.1 *Treasury estimates of government-funded 'scientific research', 1925.* £

Air Ministry (Air Force)	1,373,000
Admiralty (Navy)	983,000
War Office (Army)	495,000
DSIR	380,263
Ministry of Agriculture	348,756
Other	464,609
Total	4,044,628
Industry-funded (1930)	2,170,000

Source: R. MacLeod and K. Andrews, 'The Committee of Civil Research: advice for economic development, 1925–1930', *Minerva*, 7 (1969), p. 699. Industry funded: see Table 3.2 above.

The neglect of the military has led to a number of unfortunate impressions. The first is that the state's attitude to science and technology could be adequately gauged by its commitment to civil R&D. The second is that *war* created the circumstances which forced government to recognise the need for both civil and military R&D: in fact the British state had created powerful military-scientific complexes before both world wars [101]. The third is that the government did not support R&D in industry: in reality, the service ministries pioneered and dominated the funding of R&D in industry, for both civil and military purposes [102].

Service ministries and technical development

Before 1914 the Admiralty and the naval shipbuilders were at the centre of a scientific and industrial complex of unprecedented power [97]. As long ago as 1969 Trebilcock pointed out the importance of this complex not only for naval strength but also for the development of civil technologies [93]. He brought to the fore

Table 4.2 Government and industrial expenditure on R&D, 1964/5.
£m

Royal Navy	27.5	
Army	17.8	
Ministry of Aviation	252.4	
of which		
Work in industry*		201.7
ELDO		16.0
Launch aid, etc.		20.6
Atomic Energy (civil only)	65.3	
DSIR	25.1	
Medical Research Council	8.5	
Agriculture Research Council	8.1	
Total Government**	433.8	
Industry-funded	313.6	

Items in *italics* represent overwhelmingly civil expenditure.
*This sum was spend largely in the aircraft and electronic industries and
was overwhelmingly for military purposes. The Ministry of Aviation did
work for the Army and the Navy.
**Excluding grants to universities and learned societies which amounted
to about 30m for R&D [84:39].
Source: Estimates for 1964/5 from Civil Estimates, *PP.* 1963/4, Cmnd
2290, Vol. 23. Table VII. Industry funded as in Table 3.2 above.

the great arms firms, and their work in steel, engineering, ship-
building and motor vehicles. More recently, historians have uncov-
ered the great contribution of the Royal Navy to the development of
radio [99], and the rather convoluted story of the development of
computing devices to aim guns [100]. One reason for ignoring the
Edwardian Navy is that it did not suffer a procurement crisis in the
Great War. The army, by contrast, found it very difficult to obtain
dyestuffs, chemicals and explosives, problems seen even at the time
as an indictment of *prewar* attitudes to science [1][103]. The British
chemical industry was in some respects indeed deficient compared
to the German industry, but Britain was not intending to fight a
major land war which required its products in any quantity. In any

case, what was striking was the ability of the wartime British chemical industry to enlarge research, and to develop and produce new and old materials in vast quantities [95][103].

Aviation is the key case of a military-supported technology since in war and peace military demand dominated. Most historians have assumed that aviation was essentially civil, though with an obvious military application, for example [116]. But, the Royal Air Force of the early 1930s had hundreds of aeroplanes; Imperial Airways mere tens. The army was developing aircraft from 1906, an Advisory Committee on Aeronautics was established in 1909, and from that date R&D was supported by the state in government establishments and, indirectly, in private firms. The Air Ministry was, in the 1920s and 1930s, easily the largest government spender on R&D (see Table 4.1). Much of this expenditure was undertaken in the private aircraft industry. The usual picture of the interwar British aircraft industry is that it was backward both in quantity of output, and in terms of technical quality [13]; other studies show that it was at least as large as any in the world in the early 1930s, was probably the largest exporter, and produced aircraft of high quality [20].

In the interwar years weapons R&D and procurement was done by each of the three service ministries – the Admiralty, War Office and Air Ministry. In 1939 and 1940, however, separate Ministries of Supply (largely for the Army) and Aircraft Production were established. Breaking precedent, the Labour government of 1945 kept a separate supply ministry in peacetime, merging the two wartime ministries into one Ministry of Supply. This was, by a vast margin, the largest R&D funding institution in Britain. So too was the Ministry of Aviation which succeeded it in 1959. In the 1940s and 1950s the Ministry of Supply spent more than private industry on R&D indeed for a period the Ministry spent about the same in industry as industry did itself, as can be seen in Table 4.2 [101][103][104]. Something like half its R&D funds were spent in industry at a time when spending in industry by other ministries was negligible [103]. In addition, the Ministry of Supply was responsible for the British bomb project between 1946 and 1954; after that work was contracted out to an autonomous but publicly–owned Atomic Energy Authority [94]. The Ministry of Aviation continued to exist until 1967 when it merged into the much smaller Ministry of Technology. Only in the early 1970s did defence R&D and procurement return to the Ministry of Defence.

Expenditure on warlike R&D increased over the century. It was almost certainly greater after 1918 than before 1914. It is likely that it did not fall with the end of the Second World War, and it greatly increased in the early 1950s; thereafter Britain spent up to 15% of its defence budget on R&D [101]. It is probable that the only significant decreases were after the Great War and in the late 1960s. Britain was probably the major single source of military innovation before 1940: indeed, Britain launched the first significant programme to develop an atomic bomb [92]. In the 1940s and 1950s Britain was able to develop practically all types of military technology. But, by the late 1950s there was increasing dependence on the United States. After about 1965, with some important exceptions, Britain ceased to develop the most advanced military technologies on its own. Instead it chose to collaborate with Europe to share the hugely increasing costs of development [89][116].

Civil programmes of service and supply departments

The interwar service ministries and the postwar supply ministries, together with the Atomic Energy Authority, have been the major funders of British *civil* R&D. Before the Second World War, the Air Ministry funded development of civil aircraft [116]. After the Second World War state finance for civil R&D was highly concentrated in aerospace and nuclear power, as may be seen in Table 4.2. The postwar civil programmes were analogous to military programmes in that the first users of the technology developed were to be state enterprises: the nationalised airlines, and the nationalised electricity supply industry [85][104]. The nationalised industries did relatively little R&D themselves (see Table 3.1). There were to be controversies when the airlines or power generators wanted to purchase foreign (nearly always US) technology [85][116]. In the case of the airlines US aircraft were in much use by the 1970s; it was not until the 1980s that US nuclear technology was imported. As in the case of military technology, Britain increasingly opted out of full, independent development of large scale civil technology from the 1960s. The Concorde was an Anglo-French project; the British space programme of the 1960s was largely European. As we shall see below these postwar civil programmes have attracted a great deal of critical attention.

Other civil R&D

Arguments for the state support of research for civil industrial purposes date from the late nineteenth century. Aside from funding of higher education, museums, observatories, expeditions, and agricultural research, the government created a National Physical Laboratory (NPL) in 1900. A curious hybrid, it was funded by the Treasury and the private sector, but was controlled by the Royal Society. Its main task was establishing physical standards, but it increasingly undertook research in physics, metallurgy, engineering and aeronautics. By 1912 it was spending more than £30,000 per annum, making it a huge laboratory by the standards of the time, even though the literature on it implies (perhaps wrongly) that it was smaller than comparable institutions like the Bureau of Standards in Washington and the Physikalische-Technische Reichsanstalt in Berlin [112]. In the interwar years the NPL was spending around £200,000 per annum, and employed hundreds of staff, which made it comparable to the research efforts of some major firms, though it spent much less than ICI [113]. The NPL spawned a number of other state laboratories, including the Fuel Research Station, which did a great deal of work on converting coal to oil, work that was taken up by ICI [117], and a National Engineering Laboratory established in 1947.

During the Great War, a new Department of Scientific and Industrial Research (DSIR) was created under the Privy Council to administer both research grants for universities and a new scheme to support industrial research [87]. The latter took the form of Government grants to research associations created for this purpose. The first were formed in 1918, and 23 existed by 1924 [114]. Most remained very small indeed, but a few, like the Cotton Industry Research Association (the Shirley Institute) and the Electrical Research Association, were comparable to the laboratories of major firms. A second wave of research associations was formed in the late 1940s, the largest of which were for Production Engineering, Ship Research and Welding. In the mid-1930s the spending of research associations was about 10% of in-house industrial R&D: in 1970 it was down to about 2.5%. They were just a detail in the history of industrial research, despite the attention they have been given by historians. The best overview is [114].

The DSIR was not the only significant non-military R&D agency. The Ministry of Agriculture and Fisheries funded a great deal of research, as can be seen in Table 4.1, as did the Medical Research Council [119]. The Board of Trade also had a significant impact. Its most notable intervention was in the formation of British Dyes Ltd in the Great War, and the establishment through the company of a major research effort in organic chemistry. In the years after the war, severe import restrictions on dyestuffs had a major impact on the industry, which in the 1920s did a great deal of R&D [107]. After the Second World War, the Board of Trade under Harold Wilson established the National Research Development Corporation (sic) (NRDC) which was intended to help develop inventions made in the public or private sectors [115]. The NRDC had powers to fund private companies to develop new products which it used extensively in the case of computers and hovercraft [75:*126–7*].

In the late 1950s and early 1960s the DSIR also started funding R&D in private industry, though on a very small scale. Extending such funding became a policy commitment of the opposition Labour Party. When Labour came into office in 1964 it created a Ministry of Technology by bringing together the industrial laboratories (like the NPL) and the research associations of the DSIR, together with the NRDC and the Atomic Energy Authority. Great hopes were placed in Mintech (the Ministry was soon given this Russian-style abbreviation): it was supposed to transform the British economy by the injection of more science and technology into civil industry [90][91]. However, Mintech accounted for only about a third of government *civil* R&D, and of course, a much smaller proportion of total government R&D. Mintech was soon turned into a ministry of industry, procurement, energy, and technology by absorbing most of the industrial functions of the

Board of Trade, the whole of the Ministry of Aviation, and the Ministry of Fuel and Power. Indeed, the post-1966 Mintech was a recreation, with some variations, of the Ministry of Supply as it existed between 1945 and 1955 [90][91]. 'The white heat of the technological revolution' was Prime Minister Harold Wilson's most famous phrase, though in fact he had spoken of the 'scientific revolution' [91]. Wilson had argued for the modernisation of British industry through the injection of more R&D. However, the most striking thing about state-funded R&D between 1964 and 1970 was a very significant cut in defence R&D. Much more surprising is the fact that the Labour government came to doubt whether Britain and British industry were in fact short of civil R&D. International comparisons pointed to Britain being a high spender on civil R&D, while it had a relatively low rate of growth [91].

The debate on state-funded R&D

There are two distinct traditions of commentary on British defence R&D. The first is a complaint that the tight-fisted British Treasury, dominated by classically trained semi-pacifists, unduly restricted expenditure. Thus Barnett complained about the lack of money for aircraft development in the interwar years [13][20]. For the postwar years there is a powerful literature complaining about the cancellation of military projects like the TSR2 [89]. The second tradition, broadly but not only marxist, argues that the British state spent too much on warlike R&D in the 1930s [2] and especially in the postwar years. Indeed it has been argued that the huge military-technological effort of the British state contributed to the economic *decline* since the civil benefits were less than those of civil R&D, and because civil R&D was crowded out [9:*100–21*][25:*190–201*][96]. The argument needs to be made carefully since it is not to be confused with the view that the British state has been incapable of a technological, interventionist policy [20][25]. As we shall see in chapter 5, however, the crowding out thesis can mislead since by international standards the British government and private industry spent a great deal on civil R&D.

Table 4.3 *Government contributions to civil aircraft and engine development from 1945 to 31 March 1974. £m in 1974 prices*

	Payments	Receipts	Mid-point of project (year)
Total	1505.4	141.9	
Airframes total	741.2	54.5	
Concorde	406.8	5.8	1968
Trident	53.5	1.6	1965
Princess	47.1	nil	1951
BAC1-11	45.3	6.1	1965
Comet 1–4	38.0	12.2	1956
Brabazon	32.8	nil	1948
Engines total	764.2	87.4	
*Olympus 593	297.0	nil	1968
RB211	224.4	10.4	1971
Proteus	72.2	9.2	1950
Eland	34.8	0.1	1952

*The Olympus 593 was the engine for Concorde
Source: N.K. Gardner, 'The Economics of Launching Aid', in A. Whiting (ed.), *The Economics of Industrial Subsidies* (London, 1976), Table I, p. 153.

Both of the arguments above support the view that British governments underspent on civil R&D. By contrast neo-classical critics have focussed critical attention on the state's civil programmes. A study of 'launch aid' for civil aircraft development, which was recoverable through a levy on sales, argued that by 1974 the government had lost over £1bn (in 1974 prices), as shown in Table 4.3. On only one (small) project did government recoveries exceed payments (the Viscount turboprop airliner) but only if one ignored lost interest. 'The overall balance must be a matter of subjective judgement' wrote the author of the above assessment, but he was 'prepared to defend his belief that the net effect of aerospace launching aid has been a loss of national welfare' [109:*149*]. P.D. Henderson estimated that by 1976 the Anglo-French Concorde alone cost *Britain* £1,320m in 1975 prices. Adding interest which would otherwise have been earned gave a total cost of £2,150m. Adding likely costs beyond 1976 raised the cost to £2,290m, and including wider costs and benefits, including spin-off, revised this figure *upward* to £2,320m [110]. Comparable losses were made in civil nuclear power: the AGR programme alone produced a net loss of £2,100m to the mid-1970s [110]. These are important conclusions: Britain would have been *richer* had its government not subsidised civil aerospace and its nuclear programme. Grave as these losses were, they were almost certainly small by comparison to the losses incurred in defence R&D and procurement programmes.

Some technocratic critics have argued that these large scale civil programmes were the result of 'extraordinarily inept public decision-making' [132:69]; government should have spent more in promising areas, or spread its R&D across a wide range of industrial sectors [108]. Two objections can be made. The first is that government, scientists and engineers all genuinely believed that civil aerospace and nuclear power were *the* technologies of the future, and that Britain *had to be strong* in them to survive as an industrial nation. Governments anticipated a ready market for British aircraft and nuclear reactors, and that these markets would be of great economic significance. Secondly, it is not clear that more R&D spending in other areas would in fact have been beneficial; one should not assume that the problem with the rest of British industry was a lack of R&D, as will be argued further below [75].

We have, then, a range of views about state R&D spending. Some have argued that a lack of state spending weakened Britain; others that too much spending on the military reduced civil spending; or that misdirected civil spending reduced spending on other kinds of R&D. Depending on these views writers have come up with differing explanations of the nature of state support for technology. Those who argue that not enough was spent invoke the idea that the British state was anti-technological, usually because it was dominated by a neo-liberal Treasury with classically trained civil servants [13][89]. Some suggest that the imperial nature of the British state, which committed it to high military expenditure, led to over-expenditure on military technology [25]. A variant of this argument is that the British governments sought cheap ways of waging war by investment in a technological way of warfare [20].

Neo-liberal critics take quite a different line: they have complained that certain government departments, and the political culture more generally, were dominated by a dangerously naive enthusiasm for 'high' technology. Investments in such projects flew in the face of economic logic, and were based on arguments attractive only to the non-economist [106]. The economist P. D. Henderson has written of a 'state of mind' he called 'bipartisan technological chauvinism', which dominated discussion of technology after 1945. In this, 'mercantilism joins with patriotic sentiment, and with soap operatic visions of authentically native "sunrise industries"' [118:69–70]. Saul has complained of 'the excessively nationalistic view ... pressed with great force by engineers and scientists who believe that "the more research the better" is the only approach' [75:135]. The neo-liberal critics also attacked the lack of competition in the industries concerned, and the monopoly on advice to government by highly interested parties [106][110][111][118].

5

British technology in comparative perspective

Most studies of British technology and economic 'decline' make an explicit or implicit inter-economy comparison. Indeed, they must do so since what is at issue is *relative* not absolute decline. The quality of comparisons has generally been poor. Britain is often compared with a changing, single Other Country whose businesses are held to be larger and more scientific, whose industries are more modern, and whose state is more infused with the technocratic spirit. These Other Countries often have only a passing resemblance to real countries. To come to any sound conclusions about British technology and British economic performance we need comparisons with a number of economies carried out over the whole period under review. Furthermore, we have to compare not only investment in science and technology, but also economic performance. In this chapter I will attempt systematic inter-economy comparisons of industrial technique, higher scientific and technical education, the relations of innovation and growth, R&D expenditures, and data on innovation and patents.

Let us start with economic performance since this is what most commentators on the economic role of science and technology want to explain. As is clear from Table 5.1 Britain had the highest income per head of the major economies in 1870, was overtaken by the United States by 1913, and by Germany and France by 1973 (though only just). If we look at manufacturing labour productivity only (Table 5.2) we find that the USA was already ahead by 1875 but that Germany only overtook between 1950 and 1975. Before that British and German productivity were about the same. Unfortunately, however, such comparisons do not include

Table 5.1 *Gross domestic product per head 1870–1973. US $, 1985 prices*

	1870	1913	1950	1973
UK	2,610	4,024	5,651	10,063
USA	2,247	4,854	8,611	14,103
France	1,571	2,734	4,149	10,323
Germany	1,300	2,606	3,339	10,110
Italy	1,210	2,087	2,819	8,568
Japan	618	1,114	1,563	9,237

Source: A. Maddison, *Dynamic Forces in Capitalist Development* (Oxford, 1991).

Table 5.2 *Comparative manufacturing labour productivity, capital per worker and total factor productivity in Britain, Germany and the USA, 1875–1975*

	1875*	1899	1925*	1950	1975
Output per worker					
UK	100.0	100.0	100.0	100.0	100.0
Germany	100.0	99.0	95.2	96.0	132.9
USA	187.8	194.8	249.9	262.6	207.5
Capital per worker					
UK	100.0	100.0	100.0	100.0	100.0
Germany	60.4	97.6	61.0	77.8	107.2
USA	91.8	188.2	173.1	155.2	142.1
Total Factor Productivity					
UK	100.0	100.0	100.0	100.0	100.0
Germany	116.4	99.8	110.5	103.6	130.2
USA	189.7	166.8	218.2	235.1	183.0

*USA data for 1879 and 1929.
Source: S.N. Broadberry, 'Manufacturing and the Convergence Hypothesis: what the long-run data show', *Journal of Economic History* 53 (1993).

France, Italy or Japan, but all these countries had lower industrial efficiencies than Britain before the 1960s and 1970s.

Explaining differences in performance between economies has not proved to be a simple undertaking. Neither has it been easy to explain the growth of economies, much less comparative rates of growth. But for our purposes some results of such attempts are worth noting. For example, only a small proportion of growth can be accounted for by increases in capital and labour. Most growth appears to have come from increasing the efficiency with which both capital and labour are used, and the quality of that capital and labour. In the past this 'residual' growth (which is the same thing as growth of total factor productivity) was identified with technological progress in general, but a more refined analysis has broken down the residual into many different factors. But seeing technological progress as additional to increased supplies of capital and labour is misleading. Technological change works by dramatically changing the very character of capital and labour essentially by replacing old types of capital and labour by new types. Technological progress does not seep into existing capital and labour. If this is taken into account investment in both physical and human capital is quite central to change, and therefore to growth too.

Productivity differences in manufacturing between Britain and the USA cannot be explained by differences in inputs of capital; the USA was also well ahead in total factor productivity. Broadberry and Crafts suggest that the productivity difference is explained by large differences in human capital, proxied by wages (and not physical capital), and by the size of the US market as opposed to the British market (but not the size of plant) [121][122]. These points are important because it is often held that Britain underinvested in industry: it did by comparison with the USA, but not enough to explain the difference in productivity. Similarly Germany's postwar advantage in manufacturing productivity was not due to higher investment: Britain and Germany invested about the same in *industry* as a proportion of GDP in the postwar years, though Germany spent more on investment in total [123].

As we shall see the relations between usage of modern techniques, scientific and technical education, investment in innovation, and levels of efficiency and rates of economic growth are more complex than is often assumed in the literature which focusses on science and technology. An assessment of these relations is important in itself, but also because inferences about the state of science and technology have been drawn uncritically from data about British economic performance.

Comparative use of industrial technique

Given that British industry was less efficient in its use of both capital and labour than US industry from before the turn of the century we might well expect that the nature of technique used in the USA was different from that used in the UK. Similarly, since British industry was at about the same level of efficiency as German industry from at least the interwar years, we would expect the extent of usage same modern technique to be about the same. Equally, France, Italy and Japan should have been behind Britain, given their lower levels of productivity. Unfortunately, however, we have no systematic inter-economy comparisons of the level of technique across all industries. But it is highly unlikely that the main determinant of efficiency differences is variance in technique [30]. Britain lagged behind US levels of efficiency by some thirty years, but it is not plausible that Britain was technically behind by thirty years. On the other hand, the usage of washing machines, vacuum cleaners and refrigerators was about three decades behind in Britain, although radio and television usage was, crudely, similar [124].

Focussing on the relationship between investment and technological change is helpful in understanding relative stocks of new machines. It helps us distinguish between attitudes to investment, and attitudes to new technology, points which are too often confused. If demand for a product is not growing businesses will not add to capacity; they will use their existing machines. If, however, demand is growing, then new machines, probably of the latest type, will be added: the faster the rate of investment the larger the proportion of new machines. In both cases industrialists might well be equally technologically progressive – but the proportion of new machines actually in use will be very different. Thus probably the main reason for Chicago being more electrified than London by 1914 was that Chicago was growing very much faster: in both cases new building would be electrified, but Chicago had many more new buildings.

It seems likely that technique was used more efficiently in the United States for most of the century. The motorcar industry is a case in point [38]. For the period before 1914 it may well be that certain British industries used less machinery than foreign rivals, and were also more efficient: Lorenz has shown how British shipbuilders were less capital intensive than German, French or American, but had higher productivity [120]. It is also possible that the British cotton industry had higher productivity than that of the US despite using less efficient technique. After the Second World War the relations between usage of modern technique and productivity do not appear to be especially close [36][37]. Studies of comparative Anglo-German productivity in the 1960s and 1970s showed that there was no major difference in quality and quantity of equipment in British and German industry. These and other studies suggest that much of the productivity difference arose from inadequate use of machinery in British industry, and that this related to the technical skills of British workers and managers. For a review see [123]. It seems, therefore, though on the basis of sketchy evidence, that levels of efficiency are not determined by the technique in use, and that low productivity is not therefore evidence of poor or outdated technique. However, a great deal more research is needed on this topic [39].

Higher scientific and technical education

Skill in using machines seems to be more important than choice of machinery itself in determining productivity differences. One factor which might determine this skill is higher technical education. The most important comparison to make would be with the United States, given it was the most efficient economy in the world, but this has rarely been made. This is despite the fact that the British system of engineering education was similar to the American but quite different from that prevailing on the Continent of Europe, as Lundgreen has pointed out [125].

Historians have usually chosen to make comparisons with Germany, even though for most of our period the Germans appear to have been no more skilful at using machinery than the British. Contemporaries and historians have consistently bemoaned the lack in Britain of institutions similar to the (by 1910) eleven Technische Hochschulen of the German Empire [9][10][13]. Recent work has shown that in Britain the Technische Hochschulen model of separate engineering universities was rejected because British educationalists wished to integrate engineering education into multi-faculty universities [52]. Furthermore, where specialised institutions existed within university structures – like Imperial College and UMIST – they combined engineering with science to a much greater extent than the Technische Hochschulen. It is also worth noting that the most loudly trumpeted German success of the era, in organic chemistry, owed much more to the classically oriented German *universities* than to the Technische Hochschulen.

Quantitative comparisons between British higher technical education and the Technische Hochschulen are common, but there is no clearly established set of authoritative figures. It has been estimated that about 10,000 engineers graduated from Technische Hochschulen between 1900 and 1910, that is, about 1,000 per annum [126:*80*], while in Britain about 400 engineers were graduating per annum from a variety of institutions. In 1912/13 there were 2,686 full-time students of engineering and technology in English and Welsh universities and colleges, compared with 11,000 in Germany [41:72]. Barnett has noted of the interwar years that there was a 'colossal German superiority' in the production of graduate engineers and scientists; just before the Second World War Germany turned out 1,900 engineers while Britain could only manage 700 [13:*205*]. German production of engineers had slumped in the early 1930s, but in 1927 the Technische Hochschulen graduated no fewer than 3,500 [9:*67-87*]. The German lead is quite outstanding, even when one notes (as the literature generally does not) that between 1900 and 1945 Germany had a population some 40% larger than Britain. It seems, however, that among businessmen born after 1860 there was little difference in the proportion who had higher education (although there is no data on scientific and technical education) as Table 5.3

Table 5.3 *Higher education of a sample of English and German businessmen. Percentage with higher education, 1870–1914*

	English	German
All	13.0	24.0
Born before 1860	6.2	17.8
Born after 1860	29.7	30.6

Source: H. Berghoff and R. Möller, 'Tired Pioneers and Dynamic Newcomers? A comparative essay on English and German entrepreneurial history, 1870–1914', *Economic History Review* 47 (1994).

shows. Some historians claim that in the 1920s, and indeed before 1914, Germany was overproducing engineers [17:*113–14*].

The picture after the Second World War was very different. Britain may have enrolled a relatively low percentage of the relevant age group in higher education (as many critics have pointed out), but numbers actually graduating were high. In the mid-1950s more scientists and engineers were graduating in Britain than in Germany, as can be seen in Table 5.4. The table also shows the high proportion of British students graduating in science and technology, and the low proportion of scientists and technologists studying technology. The output of engineers was

Table 5.4 *Numbers graduating from universities and equivalent institutions in science and technology, 1954/55*

	Science and technology	% technology	Technology only*	Science and technology as % of all graduates
West Germany	6,005	54	3,243	34
Italy	5,483	43	2,358	26
GB	8,332	32	2,666	44
France	6,681	62	4,142	29

* calculated with the per cent figure.
Source: Edward McCrensky, *Scientific Manpower in Europe* (1958), Appendix III, pp. 180–1.

Table 5.5 *Proportion of age group (20–24) graduating from post-secondary education in science and technology, 1964*

	Science and Technology		Technology		Pure science	
	Univ.	Total	Univ.	Total	Univ.	Total
UK	2.3	4.6	0.79	2.74	1.4	1.72
USA	4.2	4.2	1.48	1.48	2.39	2.39
France	2.5	3.2	1.24	1.93	1.13	1.13
Germany	0.8	2.2	0.46	2.00	0.21	0.21
Japan	1.8	2.1	1.23	1.44	0.22	0.26
Italy	0.9	0.9	0.33	0.33	0.45	0.45

Source: OECD, *Gaps in Technology: Analytical Report* (Paris, 1970), Table 13, p. 38.

lower in Britain than in Germany but hardly disastrously so. By 1964, however, as Table 5.5 shows, Britain was ahead of Germany in the graduation of scientists *and* engineers at all levels. Stocks of British scientists were high too, as can be seen in Table 5.6. As a contemporary analyst put it, 'Britain has a larger stock of science graduates than any other West European country and employs a larger proportion of them in industry ... British industry, far from being short of scientists, is more richly endowed with them than is any country except the USA' [61:37]. Unfortunately we have no

Table 5.6 *Output, stock and distribution of qualified scientists. Thousands*

	Output (1963)	Stock	Distribution %		
			Industry	Service	Agriculture
USA (1959)	51.00	272	54	46	0
UK (1961)	8.70	105	31	68	1
France (1963)	8.20	42	19	80	1
Italy (1959)	3.35	103	16	84	0
Germany	1.76	–	–	–	–

Note: does not include engineers.
Source: M.C. Burstall, 'The Education of Industrial Scientists' in G. Walters and S. Cotgrove, *Scientists in British Industry* (Bath, 1967), pp. 19–46, citing OECD, *Resources of Scientific and Technical Manpower in the OECD Area* (Paris, 1964) Annex 1 Table 13, pp. 225-7.

Table 5.7 *University education of administrative elites 1970/71.*
Percentages.

	Britain	Germany	Italy
Natural science technology, etc.	26	14	10
Social science	12	17	36
Humanities and law	41	67	53
Unknown	7	2	1
No university	14	1	0
Total	100	100	100

Randomly selected from two highest civil service grades: sample nearly
one hundred for each country.
Source: Robert D. Putnam, 'Elite Transformation in Advanced Industrial
Societies: an empirical assessment of the theory of technocracy',
Comparative Political Studies 10 (1977), p. 390.

good figures for engineers, but given the levels of graduation it is
unlikely that there was a major shortfall by comparison with
Germany. If Britain was deficient in the formal training of engineers before 1939 this was no longer the case by the 1960s. It is
worth recalling that it was only in the 1960s that German manufacturing productivity was higher than British. The above account
should be compared with [57][27:*123–67*]. One particularly
striking divergence from conventional opinion is shown in Table
5.7, which shows the uniquely high proportion of scientists and
engineers in the very highest ranks of the British civil service.

Innovation and growth

Thus far we have been considering differences in levels of efficiency, technique and technical education, and have found no
clear links between them. We have not considered the comparative
evidence on innovation, or on rates of economic growth. We might
suppose that the more an economy innovates the faster it will grow
since it might create more new industries and be more likely to
change old ones. In fact, evidence from the postwar years suggests
this is not the case. In the 1960s Williams showed that high R&D-

spending countries had low rates of growth! He thought one reason for this was that high R&D countries also had very high levels of defence R&D (Britain and the USA) [127]. This argument is often, wrongly, used to downplay the significance of the conclusion, for example [15:*338*]. There was in fact no positive correlation between civil R&D spending and the rate of economic growth. For example, David Landes noted that in the early 1960s British civil R&D, in absolute terms, was running at four times the French level, but France had the higher growth rate [6:*20–1*]. R.C.O. Matthews also noted the lack of correlation between civil R&D spending (in this case relative to GNP) and economic growth. The UK spent 1.2% of GNP on economically motivated R&D in 1963 and had a growth rate of 2.5%; Japan spent 1% and had a growth rate of 8.3%; Germany spent 0.9% and had a growth rate of 4.1% [130:*7–8*]. Norris and Vaizey found a weak negative correlation between R&D spending as a proportion of GNP and growth rates [131:*123*]. See also [75:*135–7*].

Some analysts have sought to argue that there is a general relation between rates of growth and R&D spending. They see the 1950s and 1960s as exceptional, arguing that Germany and Japan were weakened by war and had access to US technology [15:*338*], or that much of the British lead was a 'statistical illusion' [9:*60*]. It has also been argued that if Britain had high R&D and low growth after the Second World War this was because of poor quality R&D, or a lack of application of that R&D [132]. Similar arguments have been made about the interwar period too [76]. The implication is that Britain was somehow unique in not translating R&D into economic growth. However the central point is that many factors determine relative rates of growth; innovation is far from being the main one.

What then about the relationship between efficiency and innovation? Williams showed that, very broadly speaking, the more efficient a country was, the more it tended to spend on R&D [130]. This conclusion has been supported by other studies. For example, Faberberg has shown that there is a strong positive correlation between rankings of GDP per capita and civil R&D/GDP, as well as patents, for the period 1960–83 [134]. Kealey has found similar correlations for both the 1960s and the 1980s [28]. From these results we might infer that since British output per head was one of the highest in the world until the 1960s, Britain should have had a good record in innovation. One reason such a conclusion seems surprising is that we too readily assume a direct link between efficiency and rates of growth. However, it is broadly the case that for the richer countries there was an inverse correlation between efficiency and rates of growth over the period 1870–1970: Japan was poor and fast-growing; Britain rich and slow-growing, leading to a convergence such that levels of efficiency in Britain and Japan are much more similar than in 1870 [27, *95–122*]. 'Catching-up' by *inefficient* economies seems to have been a more important source of growth than innovation. The inter-economy diffusion of technique played a key role.

Comparative evidence on R&D

The conclusion of the above analysis is that as an efficient, slow-growing economy Britain was probably a high R&D spender. The literature on R&D, however, suggests quite a different picture, which may be summarised as follows. Before 1914 British science-based industry and industrial R&D was weak, by comparison with Germany [76]. In the interwar years British industrial R&D was relatively underdeveloped, by contrast with the United States *and* Germany. After World War Two British R&D was deficient by comparison with the United States. By comparison with Germany and Japan it was high but was misallocated to defence and prestige civil projects, leading to weakness in bread-and-butter civil R&D, especially industrially-funded R&D [128][132][27:*123–67*].

Let us start by considering the comparison with the United States. There is evidence to suggest that before 1914 the USA was ahead of Britain: Britain then had no equivalent of the General Electric laboratory, the Bell Telephone laboratory or the Eastman Kodak laboratory. By the 1920s US industry was certainly spending much more than British industry in absolute and relative terms: US industry employed about ten times more R&D staff than British firms. Individual US firms spent more than British firms: in chemicals DuPont spent more than ICI, and in electricals GE more than GEC [80]. David Mowery has argued for a five- or sixfold difference in overall research *intensity* by comparing the

Table 5.8 *R&D intensity, UK, USA and Japan. 1930s.*

	UK	USA	Japan
(1) Industrial R&D employment as % manufacturing employment, 1933	0.03	0.18	–
(2) Industrial R&D expenditure as percent national income, late 1930s	0.15–0.29	0.5	–
(3) Total R&D expenditure as percent national income, 1934	0.3–0.4	0.6–0.7	0.22

Sources: (1) David Mowery 'Industrial Research in Britain, 1900–1950', in B. Elbaum and W. Lazonick (eds.), *The Decline of the British Economy* (Oxford, 1986), pp. 191–2; (2) Michael Sanderson, 'Research and the Firm in British Industry, 1919-39', *Science Studies*, 2 (1972), pp. 121–2; (3) Keith Pavitt, 'The Size and Structure of British Technology Activities: What we do and do not know', *Scientometrics*, 13 (1988), p. 331. Japan, from H. Odagiri and A. Goto, 'The Japanese System of Innovation' in R. Nelson (ed.), *National Innovation Systems* (New York, 1993), p. 84.

ratio of R&D employment to total employment in manufacturing [76]. However, most of the difference in intensity can be explained by differences in the productivity of labour, which was two to three times greater in the USA [14]. The comparative figures for industrial R&D expenditure as a proportion of national income suggest a twofold difference in research intensity (see Table 5.8). In the postwar years the differences between the USA and UK in R&D expenditure as a proportion of GDP were much lower than in the 1930s, as may be seen in Table 5.9 and Table 5.13. By the late 1950s, both were spending about the same in relative terms, even though in absolute terms the USA was spending five times more. By the late 1960s US industry was spending more in proportional terms. Overall, there was a relative increase in British expenditure.

Comparison with Germany is more difficult because of the lack of data before the 1950s. It is certainly correct that before the Great War the British dyestuffs industry and dyestuffs research was weak compared with Germany, but this was not a unique British phenomenon – only Germany had a German dyestuffs industry; certainly the United States did not. We do not know enough about

Table 5.9 *USA/UK comparison of R&D in manufacturing industry,*
1959. UK = 100

Absolute R&D official exchange rate (= $2.8)	1200
Absolute R&D R&D exchange rate (= $6.3)	540
Qualified scientists and engineers in R&D	490
R&D expenditure per employee	290
Qualified scientists/engineers in R&D per employee	260
R&D expenditure as % net output	180
R&D expenditure as % output	100
Labour productivity	250

Note: includes government funded R&D, in both cases representing a
similar proportion of the total, and in both cases devoted almost
exclusively to defence.
Source: C. Freeman, 'Research and Development: a comparison between
British and American industry', *National Institute Economic Review*,
No. 20, May 1962.

non-dyestuffs R&D to make a more general comparison [16].
Historians have confidently asserted that in the interwar years
German industry was doing more R&D than British industry, but
there is in fact no systematic evidence for this [80]. Impressionistic
evidence suggests that the question is open. IG Farben spent much
more than ICI, but was a larger and more diversified firm; a more
realistic comparison would pit IG Farben against ICI plus British
photographic, pharmaceutical, and synthetic fibres firms. In electrical engineering, British firms employed more R&D staff than
German firms in the 1920s [80]. No one has even claimed that
French, Italian or Japanese industry was doing more R&D than
was British industry. However, some evidence for Japan suggests
that in the 1930s it was doing a remarkably high quantity of R&D
in total, as shown in Table 5.8.

The literature on British R&D after the war strongly *implies* that
Britain underspent on industrially funded R&D compared with
Germany and Japan. The main source of this argument, and the
most refined version, is a paper by Christopher Freeman [132]. He
pointed to a British 'paradox' – British *industrial* R&D was high in
the 1960s, and yet Britain had a low rate of growth. Freeman
resolved the paradox by pointing out that British industry spent a
very high proportion of this *industrial* R&D on aeronautical and

Table 5.10 *Estimated distribution of industrial R&D expenditure 1962. Percentages*

	UK	France	Germany*	Japan*	USA
Aircraft	35.4	27.7	–	–	36.3
Vehicles and machinery	10.3	9.0	19.2	12.7	15.6
Electrical machinery/ Instruments	24.0	25.7	33.8	28.0	25.5
Chemicals	11.6	16.8	32.9	28.3	12.6

* 1963

Source: C. Freeman, 'Technical Innovation and British Trade Performance', in F.T. Blackaby (ed.), *De-Industrialisation* (London, 1978), p. 67.

Table 5.11 *Sectoral distribution of privately funded industrial R&D, 1969 or 1970. Percentages*

	USA 1970	Japan 1970	Germany 1969	France 1970	UK 1969
Aerospace	11.8	–	0.1	7.8	1.1
Electrical/electronic	19.5	24.9	29.3	16.5	20.4
Instruments/machinery/ Computers	19.6	13.8	8.6	–	14.8
Vehicles/shipbuilding, other	12.4	11.6	16.7	14.6	11.7
Total engineering	63.3	50.3	54.7	–	48.0
Chemicals/drugs/ petroleum prod.	20.3	22.7	33.1	24.2	22.1
Total ALL industry	100.0	100.0	100.0	100.0	100.0

Source: OECD, *OECD Science and Technology Indicators: resources devoted to R&D* (Paris, 1984), Table 2.39, p. 121, and Table 2.43, p. 127.

other state-funded projects. His figures are shown in Table 5.10. The implication was that subtracting aeronautical and state funded R&D would have left British industry with less R&D than Germany or Japan [132]. Unfortunately for the argument this was not the case in absolute terms until the late 1960s, and in relative terms not until the 1970s, as may be seen in Tables 5.12 and 5.13. If we look at *industry-funded* R&D, and thus exclude most defence and civil prestige projects, Britain did more R&D than its non-

Table 5.12 *Relative levels of absolute industry-funded industrial R&D 1963 and 1973. USA=100*

	1963	1973
USA	100.0	100.0
UK	15.6 (1964)	9.8
Germany	14.5 (1964)	17.5
Japan	10.7	23.6
France	10.3 (1966)	10.7
Italy	3.3	4.4*

* 1972

Source: OECD data reported in Keith Pavitt and Michael Worboys, *Science, Technology and the Modern Industrial State* (London, 1977), Table 6.

Table 5.13 *R&D financed by manufacturing industry as percentage of domestic product of manufacturing industry*

	1967	1969	1973
USA	3.53	3.77	3.83
UK	3.27	3.04	2.59*
Japan	2.38	2.7	3.01
Germany	2.23	2.3	2.34

*1972

Source: OECD figures in K. Pavitt and Luc Soete, 'Innovative Activities and Export Shares: some comparisons between industries and countries' in K. Pavitt (ed.), *Technical Innovation and British Economic Performance* (London, 1980), p. 60.

USA competitors [135]. Indeed, the sectoral distribution of *industry-funded* R&D is much the same in all the major countries (see Table 5.11).

These figures also cast doubt on the argument (discussed in chapter 4) that defence and aeronautical R&D had a damaging effect on the British economy. British industry did not underspend on civil R&D if we assume, as we should, that most industry-funded R&D was done for civil purposes. Military R&D took place on top of a substantial civil effort. However, the effect of the large defence R&D sector may well have been damaging not because it reduced civil R&D, but because it reduced the numbers of scientists and engineers working in non-R&D functions in industry.

It seems that the comparative story of R&D mirrors the story of industrial efficiency; Britain spent what we would expect a rich country to spend. In fact it did not do so exactly: in the 1960s Germany was wealthier than Britain, and yet Britain did more industrial R&D; France also overtook Britain in wealth, and did so doing even less R&D. In the late 1960s German and Japanese firms pushed their R&D expenditures much higher than British levels in absolute terms, and later in relative terms too. However, French and Italian firms continued to spend less than British firms in both absolute and relative terms, and yet both are now more efficient economies than Britain [135]. It seems that, if anything, Britain spent more on civil R&D than its wealth indicated, at least in the postwar years.

The evidence from patents and innovation

A great difficulty arises in comparing patent data internationally: countries used very different criteria in granting patents. For this reason comparative patenting in the USA has been used instead, even though it is not obvious that innovators of different countries had an equal propensity to patent in the USA. Into the early 1960s Britain and Germany dominated foreign patenting in the USA. France came a poor third, and Italy and Japan were very minor patenters. In the 1960s and 1970s this altered dramatically with Japan overtaking first France, then Britain (in the late 1960s), and then Germany [9:43]. Table 5.14 gives the relative patenting in the USA of British and German residents. If we exclude war years, which saw German patenting in the USA stopping, we see that the period between the 1880s and the 1960s saw a constant relative decline of the British position. If, however, we include postwar

Table 5.14 *Ratio of UK/Germany patents in the
USA, 1886–1965 (Germany=100)*

	Patents	Population	Patents per capita
1886–90	160	76	210
1901–5	100	72	138
1910–15	80	68	117
1924–6*	100+	71	140+
1936–40	60	69	86
1955–8*	100+	96	104+
1965	60	92	65

Source: K. Pavitt and Luc Soete, 'Innovative Activities
and Export Shares: some comparisons between
industries and countries' in K. Pavitt, *Technical
Innovation and British Economic Performance* (London,
1980), p. 43. *Figures not given in source: taken here
from graph. Population from Maddison.

years the picture looks somewhat different, though this may not
reflect German inventiveness, only German US patenting. If we
take population into account the British relative decline is even
more striking. However, the relative positions are somewhat
different: Britain patented more per capita in the USA than did
Germany before 1914. In the interwar years Britain patented more
in the 1920s, Germany more in the 1930s: overall patenting per
capita was about the same. For the postwar years Britain is clearly
in the lead until the late 1950s.

As Cantwell has shown, German patents were highly concentrated in chemicals [136]. It may well be that chemicals was a more
patent-intensive sector in terms of patents per innovation, and
indeed that the German chemical companies pursued an especially
patent-intensive strategy [78:*135–50*]. For the interwar years IG
Farben accounted for more than 16% of all German patents in the
USA, while ICI accounted for less than 4% of British US patents;
indeed IG patented six times more than ICI in the interwar years
[137]. And yet IG did not have six times ICI's researchers; the
difference was about twofold [80]. In terms of patents it is
plausible that Germany had an advantage in *patenting* due to

Table 5.15 *Major inventions, discoveries and innovations by country (as percent of total)*

	Total	Britain	France	Germany	USA	Other
1876–1900	204	14.2	17.2	19.1	37.7	11.8
1901–1925	139	13.7	9.4	15.1	52.5	9.4
1926–1950	113	11.5	0.9	12.4	61.9	13.3

Source: Data calculated from Clarence K. Streit, *Union Now: a proposal for an Atlantic Federal Union of the Free*, 2nd edn (New York, 1949), in K. Pavitt, and L. Soete., 'International Differences in Economic Growth and the International Location of Innovation', in H. Giersch (ed.), *Emerging Technologies* (Tubingen, 1982), p. 107. Note the small sample of innovations, and the fact that the table is not corrected for population. British population was considerably smaller than German, and the population of the USA grew especially fast over the period.

concentration on chemistry, and its pursuing of a patent-gaining strategy in chemistry. On the other hand, it may be that German patenting in the USA underrepresented German invention in the 1920s. In short, the detail of the picture is unclear. But we should beware the argument that specialisation of patents in 'modern' industries is a measure of technological strength. Cantwell identifies the relative concentration of patents in a particular sector with 'advantage', but this specialisation index, while it may be an index of *comparative* advantage, is not an index of *absolute* advantage in technology. Italy may have had a comparative advantage in aviation, that is to say it was better at inventing in aviation than in chemistry, but it does not mean that it was good at inventing in either aviation or chemicals by world standards [137].

Comparisons with Germany, France, Japan and Italy miss by far the most important technological power of the twentieth century: the United States itself. A huge majority of the products and processes which characterise the post-1945 world are of American origin: in technology, as in so much else, this has indeed been the American century. American industry as a whole, and individual American firms, have been the key benchmark against which technologists in other countries have had to measure themselves. An OECD study of 110 significant innovations from 1945 to the early 1960s showed that 74 were American, but only 18 British, 14

German and 2 French [129:*198*]. These, and other inventions and innovations, were used abroad, for which the USA received payments in licences and royalties. In the late 1950s and early 1960s the United States had a huge positive balance of payments in patents and licences. OECD calculated these rough ratios of receipts to payments: USA (1956), 5.9; UK (1964), 1.1; Germany (1963), 0.4; France (1963), 0.4 [129:*203*]. According to another listing (Table 5.15) the USA was ahead from before 1900! The most striking change shown in Table 5.15 is the collapse of the French position, but both Britain *and* Germany also show a relative decline.

6
Conclusions

Once we recognise that the relative decline of Britain is not to be equated with doing badly, the conclusions arising from this pamphlet will not appear so surprising. Until the 1960s Britain was the second richest large industrial economy in the world. And it had science and technology to match. This was true both of the education of scientists and engineers, especially after 1945, and of innovation. From 1870 to the late 1960s its innovative record was better than or comparable to that of Germany, its main rival other than the United States.

The picture given in the literature on British science and technology is consistently different. The technocratic literature has argued that technical experts were few in number and of low status in Britain, and this had disastrous consequences for economic performance; we have shown that this tradition has given us a thoroughly misleading picture of science and technology in Britain. Neo-Schumpeterian critics have overestimated the significance of innovation to national economic performance. They have also thoroughly underestimated British efforts in this area. As we have shown, David Mowery's influential account of British industrial R&D before 1950 underplays the significance of in-house industrial R&D, and exaggerates British backwardness compared to the USA. Marxist accounts rightly stress the significance of military R&D: it was always more significant than state-funded civil R&D, especially in industry. Indeed the strength of military R&D vitiates most of the general comments made about state funding of R&D. Nevertheless, by underestimating the strength of industry-funded R&D, marxist critics have wrongly suggested that military R&D took place at the expense of civil R&D.

Neo-classical analysts have helped to change our picture radically. Their international comparisons of efficiency have made clear exactly what is to be explained. By doing this they have shown that many historians of science and technology have been trying to explain something which was not the case; for example that Britain was behind Germany, or that British industry was short of capital. Similarly, economists have shown that innovation is not the main determinant of differences in rates of economic growth, thus undermining the common argument that because Britain grew relatively slowly it must have (1) underspent on innovation, or (2) misdirected its innovation. The conclusions of neo-classical analysis open the history of British science and technology to fresh questions, even if we might doubt the more general applicability of neo-classical methods. In particular it helps us break decisively with the influential assumptions of scientists and engineers on the economic role of science and technology. This is somewhat surprising since the cliometric tradition is often seen as applying the methods of science to the humanities, and therefore unlikely to be a good method of analysis of science and technology.

Historiographical fashion has led to a mistrust of quantitative history, and even economic history more generally. In the case of the British decline, new quantification and economic thinking has been the decisive influence in changing the terms of the debate. This is very important for the history of British science and technology, since it has too often been discussed in the context of a peculiarly declinist account of economic history. It is worth stressing that this declinist historiography of British science and technology has been primarily cultural, as exemplified in the work of C.P. Snow, Martin Wiener and Correlli Barnett. The problem of science and technology in Britain is seen primarily as a cultural problem, in that culture was not receptive enough to science and technology. An anti-declinist account of British science and technology points to an alternative cultural history of British science. We might ask, for example, why the declinist cultural account of British science and technology since 1870 has held our imaginations in such an iron grip. A very few commentators have addressed this issue. But it seems that scientists and engineers themselves were the key propagators of the argument. Convinced that *national* investments in science and technology are the key sources of *national* economic power, they necessarily explained what they saw as deficiencies in economic power by a lack of science and technology or its misapplication (often failing to distinguish between science and technology in general and innovation). It is a measure of the influence of scientists and engineers in British intellectual life that these arguments have had such influence, not least on economic and social historians (of many varieties). The pervasiveness of the techno-declinist position is evidence of the high esteem in which scientists and engineers are held. This paradoxical conclusion about ideas parallels another about policy. Despite constant arguments that scientists and engineers had more influence in other countries, British higher education, the British state, and British industry were, if anything, peculiarly scientific and technological.

This small book has had to survey a large literature. But the reader going on to explore this literature should be warned that reading some of it can be a very frustrating and dispiriting experience. Making sense of it requires critical attention being given to what is being explained, the assumptions employed, and the explanations given. It is particularly important to be aware of implicit definitions used, the accuracy and representativeness of international comparisons, and the plausibility of the overall picture presented. It is often helpful to ask whether the opposite of what is stated and implied in much of the literature might be closer to an adequate historical picture than that presented. Certainly, it has been the argument of this book that this has too often been the case, but it is up to the reader to judge. What is abundantly clear, however, is that there is now more than one account of the relations between science, technology, and the British industrial 'decline'.

Glossary

Development. The refinement and improvement of an existing or new product or process. Usually includes the design and building of pilot plants and prototypes.

Diffusion. The increasing use of a technique, often measured as the percentage of maximum use achieved. Inventions and innovations only acquire economic importance when they have diffused. However, the extent of usage is not an adequate measure of economic impact.

Efficiency. The extent to which inputs are turned into outputs, for example the amount produced per worker, or labour *productivity* (qv). Thus GDP per capita (that is, per person) is a measure of efficiency, as well as the most convenient general measure of living standards. The level of efficiency does not determine the rate of *growth* (qv).

Government-funded R&D. Government-funded R&D was principally concerned with warfare; only from the late 1960s was it equally divided between civil and military sectors. Only a minority of government funds for R&D were spent by government itself: most went to industry. See Industrial R&D.

Gross Domestic Product. The total output of an economy measured by summing expenditures, incomes, or outputs.

Growth. The growth of an economy or industry is usually measured as the increase in production over a year, as a percentage of the production of the previous year. Should not be confused with the amount of production, or the *efficiency* (qv) of production.

Industrial R&D. This is the total of R&D carried out in industry. The overwhelming majority is carried out in *manufacturing* (qv) industry. The main sources of funds were industry itself (overwhelmingly for civil purposes) and, secondly, government, most of which was for defence. Not all R&D is 'industrial R&D'. Government itself carries out R&D in its own establishments, as do universities.

Industry. A surprisingly ambiguous term. In the standard British definition of economic activity industry (manufacturing plus energy and water) is distinguished from agriculture, construction and services (which includes transport and communications).

Industry-funded R&D. Here taken to mean industry's own funding of its own R&D. This was very largely for civil purposes and highly concentrated in manufacturing.

Innovation. The first use of an *invention* (qv).

Invention. An original idea or device, sometimes described in and protected by a *patent* (qv).

Manufacturing. That part of *industry* (qv) which makes things (for example newspapers or pottery), but excludes important sectors like energy and water supply. Should not therefore be equated with the whole of industry, much less the whole economy.

Patent. A legal document granted to an inventor which details the invention, which is thus made public, and grants a temporary monopoly on its use.

Polytechnic. Higher education institutions created in the late 1960s by merging local authority *technical colleges* (qv) with other colleges. Remained under the control of local authorities until the 1980s, when they were first given independent corporate status. In the 1990s most became *universities* (qv).

Productivity. The output of an economy, industrial sector, or firm (etc.), divided by an input, usually labour (number of workers, or the number of hours worked), giving labour productivity, or capital (giving capital productivity). Total Factor Productivity is a measure of the joint productivity of both capital and labour, which is also known as the 'residual'. Not to be confused with production, which measures total output only. Like output figures, productivity is often given as annual percentage change in productivity, which should not be confused with levels of productivity.

Research. Original investigation, usually of a scientific or technical nature.

Research and development (R&D). Organised, team-based scientific and technical *research* (qv) and *development* (qv). Since development typically accounts for much more than research, it should more accurately be called 'development and research'. Large firms often had, and have, separate facilities for research and for development. R&D was a very minor source of *invention* (qv) or *innovation* (qv) around 1900, but a major, though not the only source by 1970. It is thus not an especially good measure of inputs into invention and innovation. A minority of scientists and technologists, even of those employed in industry, have been engaged in R&D.

Service ministries. Only since 1964 has the Ministry of Defence been responsible for all the armed services. Before then each had a separate ministry: the War Office for the Army, the Admiralty for the Navy, and, from 1918, the Air Ministry for the RAF. Each of these ministries carried out R&D and procurement, except when these functions were given to specialist *supply ministries* (qv).

Supply Ministries. Ministries devoted to R&D and procurement for one or more of the *service ministries* (qv). In 1915–21 the Ministry of Munitions of War supplied the army; in 1939–45 the Ministry of Supply took over this function, while the Ministry of Aircraft Production, 1940–5, did the same for the air force. Between 1945 and 1959 the Ministry of Supply was the major procurement and R&D organisation for the forces, followed by the Ministry of Aviation (1959–67) and the Ministry of Technology (1967–70).

Technical College. A post-school centre of technical education usually owned and run by a local authority. In the 1950s some were designated as Colleges of Advanced Technology and later removed from the control of local authorities, becoming *universities* (qv) in the late 1960s. Many of the remainder were incorporated into the *polytechnics* (qv) created in the 1960s.

Technology. A confusing term which originally meant the study of technique. Now it usually means both the study of technique, and technique itself. The technological level of nations is extremely difficult to measure. One possible indication is the level of *efficiency* (qv), but the most common measure is based on rates of *invention* (qv) or *innovation* (qv). This is misleading since invention and innovation are measures of the rate of development of new technology, not of the quality or quantity of technique in use.

University. An independent teaching body with the power to award degrees. Conventionally divided into Ancient (sometimes rightly including Edinburgh, Glasgow, St Andrews, and Aberdeen), the 'civics' or 'redbricks' (usually including London and Durham), the former Colleges of Advanced Technology, and the entirely new 'plate glass' universities of the 1960s. All the above are now known as the 'old universities', to distinguish them from the 'new universities' created from *polytechnics* (qv).

Bibliography

Journals

Articles relevant to the topic discussed here are widely distributed in many different journals covering different fields of enquiry: economic and business history (*Business History* (*Bus. Hist.*), *Business History Review*, *Economic History Review* (*Econ. Hist. Rev.*), *Journal of Economic History*); history of science (*Annals of Science, British Journal for the History of Science, Historical Studies in the Physical and Biological Sciences, History of Science, Isis*); history of technology (*History and Technology, History of Technology, Technology and Culture*); history of education (*History of Education*); and economic, social and political studies of science and technology (*Minerva, Research Policy, Science and Public Policy, Scientometrics, Social Studies of Science* (previously *Science Studies*)).

The following highly selective bibliography is arranged by category, and within categories in broadly chronological order, to give some picture of the historical development of the literature. However, the bibliography is heavily weighted towards recent works, and I have tended to omit works easily accessible through bibliographies in other works listed. I have indicated works which contain useful bibliographies.

Introduction and general

[1]   Sir John Clapham, *An Economic History of Modern Britain: machines and national rivalries (1887-1914)* (Cambridge, 1938). See Chapter 3 for a detailed but broadly optimistic story of British industrial and technical development.

[2]   J.D. Bernal, *The Social Function of Science* (London, 1939). A pioneering account of the funding of British science and technology. A marxist work, it argued that monopolies retarded industrial research, and that British science was highly weighted towards the military. Better informed about industry than most later commentators. On Bernal see [7] [11].

[3]   D.S.L. Cardwell, *The Organisation of Science in England* (London, 1957, 1972).

[4]   C.P. Snow, *The Two Cultures and the Scientific Revolution* (Cambridge, 1959). Although not usually thought of in this way it is essentially a work of bad history; indeed it is an exemplar of 1950s social history of British science. To be compared with [10] and [13].

[5]   H.J. Habakkuk, *American and British Technology in the 19th Century: the search for labour-saving inventions* (Cambridge, 1962). Chapter 6 concerns Britain in the late nineteenth century, and rejects the idea that Britons were unentrepreneurial or uninnovative.

[6]   D. Landes, *The Unbound Prometheus: technological change and industrial development in Western Europe from 1750 to the present* (Cambridge, 1969). Pioneering and unsurpassed techno-economic history. Much concerned with Schumpeterian themes and, for the period since 1870, with the British decline. For criticism see [18].

[7]   Gary Werskey, *The Visible College* (London, 1978, 1988). A history of the socialist scientists of the 1930s and their ideas and influence.

[8]   Frank Turner, 'Public Science in Britain', *Isis*, 71 (1980). A pioneering article, which shows the origins of declinism in the scientific community. Stresses that scientists' public pronouncements are not to be taken as evidence of their actual position in society.

[9]   Keith Pavitt (ed.), *Technical Change and British Economic Performance* (London, 1980). Collection of articles giving a consistently declinist perspective on British technology. By far the best source for the standard argument that British science and technology (notably innovation) was deficient after 1945, with negative consequences for the British economy. Certainly, far superior in this respect to Wiener and Barnett. Note in particular the article by Pavitt and Soete (38–66) which deals largely with the period after 1967, the article by Albu (67–87) on engineers, which still remains the best long-range comparison between British and German engineering, and the article by Kaldor on defence technology (100–24).

[10]   Martin Wiener, *English Culture and the Decline of the Industrial Spirit* (Cambridge, 1981). Only one chapter deals with higher education as such. Nevertheless, very influential. For critiques see [16][17][18][20][23].

[11]   W. McGucken, *Scientists, Society and the State: The Social Relations of Science Movement in Great Britain, 1931–1947* (Columbus, Ohio, 1984).

[12]   Bernard Elbaum and William Lazonick (eds.), *The Decline of the British Economy* (Oxford, 1986). Neo-Schumpeterian argument for an 'institutional' understanding. The chapter on technical education is a classic piece of declinism; the treatment of industrial R&D

is misleading. Contains a number of examples of the thesis that craft control dominated in British industry. For a general critique see [18]; for critiques of the treatment of technical education and R&D see [16] and [80] respectively.

[13] Correlli Barnett, *The Audit of War: the illusion and reality of Britain as a great nation* (London, 1986). Easily the most influential work on technology and the British decline of the past decade. Stressed technical and industrial failure during the Second World War, and traced this, in large part, to problems dating from the 1870s in scientific and technical education. For critiques see [17] and [21].

[14] D.E.H. Edgerton, 'Science and Technology in British Business history', *Bus. Hist.*, 29 (1987). A critical review of the usefulness of business histories as sources for the history of industrial research and of the arguments about science and technology in British business.

[15] Keith Pavitt, 'The Size and Structure of British Technology Activities: what we do and do not know', *Scientometrics* 13 (1988). Useful general survey of the work of the science policy tradition on the history of British R&D, invention and innovation. Contains an extensive bibliography.

[16] Sidney Pollard, *Britain's Prime and Britain's Decline* (London, 1989). Chapter 3, the length of a short book, is an extended comparison of British and German science, technology and education before 1914. It demolishes the argument that Britain was well behind Germany in technical education before 1914, and stresses growth in British technical education. Contains an extensive bibliography.

[17] Bruce Collins and Keith Robbins (eds.), *British Culture and Economic Decline* (London, 1990). A devastating critique of the Barnett/Wiener thesis, with articles by William Rubinstein, Peter Payne, Harold James and Bruce Collins.

[18] Donald McCloskey, 'The Politics of Stories in Historical Economics', in *If You're So Smart* (Chicago, 1990). One of the few articles to enquire into the intellectual history of declinism, and its characteristic arguments. Essential reading.

[19] Bill Luckin, *Questions of Power* (Manchester, 1990). A study of the cultural context of British electrification.

[20] David Edgerton, *England and the Aeroplane: an essay on a militant and technological nation* (London, 1991). A contribution to the debate on the British state and economic decline. Argues for the strength of British aviation and for the centrality of a particular warlike strategy. Argues that England was a warfare, as well as a welfare, state. A study of the Right from the Left.

[21] David Edgerton, 'The Prophet Militant and Industrial: the pecula-

rities of Correlli Barnett', *Twentieth Century British History* 2 (1991). A critique of Barnett which deals not with the welfare state but with Barnett's central arguments: education, technology and war. Also reviews the reviews of Barnett, showing that most historians agreed with him on education and technology. Takes Barnett as an exemplar of the technocratic (and militaristic) critiques of modern Britain.

[22]   William Lazonick, *Business Organization and the Myth of the Market Economy* (Cambridge, 1991). Argues for a neo-Schumpeterian view of twentieth century capitalist development. Contains an intellectual history of the influence of Schumpeter and Schumpeterian ideas on other such Harvard alumni and teachers such as David Landes, Alfred Chandler and William Lazonick. J.K. Galbraith is, surprisingly, given little attention.

[23]   W.D. Rubinstein, *Capitalism, Culture and Economic Decline in Britain, 1750–1990* (London, 1993). Essentially a collection of long essays, the two central ones are a devastating critique of the cultural critique (in largely cultural terms) and a study of the relations of business and the public schools. Confuses the cultural critique with what he sees as the erroneous view that Britain was an industrial country. While it is true that industrial production was never as important in creating fortunes, or in terms of employment, as some have implied, nevertheless industrial output has been a very significant part of total output, and by comparison with other countries Britain has indeed been an industrial economy. Even if Britain was an industrial nation the cultural critique is still wrong; the two arguments are independent.

[24]   J.V. Pickstone, 'Ways of Knowing: towards a historical sociology of science, technology and medicine', *British Journal for the History of Science* 26 (1993).

[25]   David Coates, *The Question of UK Decline: the economy, state and society* (London, 1994). The best treatment of the arguments about the decline since 1945 since it differentiates between them along political/ideological lines. Contains extensive bibliography.

[26]   R. Floud and D.N. McCloskey, *The Economic History of Britain since 1700*, second edition, Vol. II *1860–1939* (Cambridge, 1994). See in particular the papers by Pollard on entrepreneurship (62–89), Lazonick on employment relations (90–116) and Foreman-Peck on industry in the interwar years (386–414).

[27]   R. Floud and D.N. McCloskey, *The Economic History of Britain since 1700*, second edition, Vol. III *1939–1992* (Cambridge, 1994). See in particular the papers by Feinstein (95–122), Millward (123–67) and Supple (318–46).

[28]   Terence Kealey, *The Economic Laws of Scientific Research* (Basing-

stoke, 1995). Neo-liberal historical and economic account of scientific research which argues that economic development determines expenditure on, and quality of science. Government funding, it is argued, reduces total funding of R&D. A real challenge to conventional views. As the work of a scientist to be compared with [2][4].

Technique in use

[29] D.N. McCloskey (ed.), *Essays on a Mature Economy: Britain after 1840* (London, 1971). Pioneering articles on the diffusion of technique in British industry before 1914, and its economic significance.

[30] D.N. McCloskey, *Enterprise and Trade in Victorian Britain* (London, 1981). A collection of the author's papers, including historical accounts of the development of historical economics, and key papers attacking the 'entrepreneurial failure' thesis.

[31] Lars Sandberg, 'The Entrepreneur and Technological Change', in R. Floud and D.N. McCloskey (eds.), *The Economic History of Britain since 1700* Vol. I, first edition (Cambridge, 1981).

[32] D.C. Coleman and C. MacLeod, 'Attitudes to New Techniques: British businessmen 1800-1950', *Econ. Hist. Rev.* 39 (1986).

[33] W. Lazonick, 'Factor Costs and the Diffusion of Ring Spinning in Britain prior to World War I', *Quarterly Journal of Economics* 96 (1981).

[34] W. Lazonick, 'Industrial Organisation and Technological Change: the decline of the British cotton industry', *Business History Review* 57 (1983). Important statement of a general thesis developed in [12]. Distinguishes clearly between management and entrepreneurship.

[35] D.M. Higgins, 'Rings, Mules and Structural Constraints in the Lancashire Textile Industry, c. 1945–c.1965', *Econ. Hist. Rev.* 46 (1993). Readers should refer back from this paper to the debates between Lazonick and Saxonhouse and Wright.

[36] L. Nasbeth and G.F. Ray, *The Diffusion of New Industrial Processes* (Cambridge, 1974).

[37] G.F. Ray, *The Diffusion of Mature Technologies* (Cambridge, 1984). Follow up to [36].

[38] Wayne Lewchuk, *American Technology and the British Motor Vehicle Industry* (Cambridge, 1987).

[39] Jonathan Zeitlin, *Between Flexibility and Mass Production* (Oxford, forthcoming).

Higher scientific and technological education

[40] G.L. Payne, *Britain's Scientific and Technological Manpower* (Stanford, 1960). This work contains probably the best description of the higher education of scientists and engineers in the 1940s and 1950s, as well as a wealth of statistics.

[41] Michael Argles, *South Kensington to Robbins: an account of English technical and scientific education since 1851* (London, 1964).

[42] K.G. Gannicot and M. Blaug, 'Manpower Forecasting since Robbins: a science lobby in action', *Higher Education Review* 2 (1969).

[43] Michael Sanderson, *The Universities and British Industry, 1850–1970* (London, 1972). Still by far the best study of scientific and technological studies in British universities. Although published long before the key works of Barnett and Wiener, it demolished their arguments in advance.

[44] P.L. Robertson, 'Technical Education in the British Shipbuilding and Marine Engineering Industries 1863–1914', *Econ. Hist. Rev.*, 27 (1974).

[45] G. Roderick and M. Stephens, 'Scientific Studies and Scientific Manpower in the English Civic Universities, 1870–1914', *Science Studies* 4 (1974).

[46] R. Kargon, *Science in Victorian Manchester: enterprise and expertise* (Manchester, 1977).

[47] Margaret Gowing, 'Science, Technology and Education: England in 1870', *Oxford Review of Education* 4 (1978). A good example of the classic declinist position on technical education.

[48] Michael Sanderson, 'The Professor as Industrial Consultant: Oliver Arnold and the British steel industry, 1900–1914', *Economic History Review* 37 (1978).

[49] P.L. Robertson, 'Scottish Universities and Industry, 1860–1914', *Scottish Economic and Social History* 4 (1984).

[50] Michael Sanderson, 'The English Civic Universities and the "industrial spirit", 1870-1914', *Historical Research* 61 (1988). A devastating critique of Wiener's treatment of higher education.

[51] Crosbie Smith and M. Norton Wise, *Energy and Empire: a biographical study of Lord Kelvin* (Cambridge, 1989).

[52] P. Hennock, 'Technological Education in England, 1850–1926: the uses of a German model', *History of Education*, 19 (1990). An important article by a scholar who knows Britain and Germany. Describes the conscious British rejection of the German model.

[53] Colin Divall, 'A Measure of Agreement: employers and engineering studies in the universities of England and Wales, 1897–1939', *Social Studies of Science*, 20 (1990).

[54] Graeme Gooday, 'Precision Measurement and the Genesis of

physics teaching laboratories in Victorian Britain', *British Journal for the History of Science* 23 (1990).

[55]   Graeme Gooday, 'Teaching Telegraphy and Electrotechnics in the Physics Laboratory: William Ayrton and the creation of an academic space for electrical engineering in Britain. 1873–1884', *History of Technology* 13 (1991).

[56]   G. Tweedale, 'Geology and Industrial Consultancy: Sir William Boyd Dawkins (1837–1929) and the Kent coalfield', *British Journal for the History of Science* 24 (1991).

[57]   D.H. Aldcroft, *Education, Training and Economic Performance, 1944–1990* (Manchester, 1992). The most comprehensive general treatment, notable for the review of the literature on the relationship between education and economic performance. Misleading and self-contradictory about the development of British higher scientific and technological education.

[58]   Simon Schaffer, 'Late Victorian Metrology and its Instrumentation: a manufactory of ohms', in R. Bud and S.E. Cozzens, *Invisible Connections: instruments, institutions and science* (Washington, 1992).

Experts in Industry

[59]   Bosworth Monck, 'The Eclipse of the Engineer in Management', *Engineering* 10 September 1954, pp. 329–34.

[60]   Charlotte Erickson, *British Industrialists, Steel and Hosiery 1850–1950* (Cambridge, 1959).

[61]   M.C. Burstall, 'The Education of Industrial Scientists', in G. Walters and S. Cotgrove, *Scientists in British Industry* (Bath, 1967).

[62]   G.S. Bain, *The Growth of White-Collar Unionism* (Oxford, 1970).

[63]   D.C. Coleman, 'Gentlemen and Players', *Econ. Hist. Rev.* 26 (1973). An influential, though essentially preliminary study which anticipated many of the complaints of Barnett and Wiener.

[64]   D.C. Coleman, 'Failings and Achievements: some British businesses, 1910–80'. *Bus. Hist.* 27 (1987).

[65]   Ian Glover and Michael Kelly, *Engineers in Britain: a sociological study of the engineering dimension* (London, 1987). Contains extensive bibliography.

[66]   G. Tweedale, *Sheffield Steel and America* (Cambridge, 1987). An important work which strongly defended the Sheffield industry from charges of technical backwardness.

[67]   Angus Buchanan, *The Engineers: a history of the engineering profession in Britain, 1750–1914* (London, 1989).

[68]   James Donnelly, 'Industrial Recruitment of Chemists from English Universities: a reevaluation of its early importance', *British Journal for the History of Science* 24 (1991).

[69]   James Donnelly, 'Consultants, Managers and Testing Slaves: changing roles for chemists in the British alkali industry, 1850–1920', *Technology and Culture* 35 (1994).

[70]   S.M. Horrocks, 'Quality Control and Research: the role of scientists in the British food industry, 1870–1939', in John Burnett and Derek J. Oddy (eds.), *The Origins and Development of Food Policies in Europe* (Leicester, 1994).

[71]   Andrew Pettigrew, *The Awakening Giant: continuity and change in Imperial Chemical Industries* (Oxford, 1985). Revealing study of managerial change in ICI.

Industrial R&D (see also the Comparative section below)

[72]   C.F. Carter and B.R. Williams, *Industry and Technical Progress: factors governing the speed of application of Science* (London, 1957).

[73]   Michael Sanderson, 'Research and the firm in British industry, 1919–39', *Science Studies*, 2 (1972). A classic article which refuted Mowery [76] long before the latter appeared.

[74]   Leslie Hannah, *The Rise of the Corporate Economy* (London, 1976, 2nd edn 1983). Gives an appropriately upbeat account of interwar industrial R&D.

[75]   S.B. Saul, 'Research and Development in British Industry from the end of the nineteenth century to the 1960s', in T.C. Smout (ed.), *The Search for Wealth and Stability* (London, 1979). A very useful, judicious survey, which argued that Britain was good at innovation, especially after 1945. One of the few historical treatments of industrial innovation after 1945. Casts doubt on the crowding out thesis.

[76]   David Mowery, 'Industrial Research in Britain, 1900–1950', in B. Elbaum and W. Lazonick (eds.), *The Decline of the British Economy* (Oxford, 1986). Influential article, criticised in [14][80] [81].

[77]   Keith Pavitt, M. Robson and S. Townsend, 'The Size Distribution of Innovating Firms in the UK, 1945–1983', *Journal of Industrial Economics* 35 (1987).

[78]   Jonathan Liebenau (ed.), *The Challenge of New Technology: innovation in British business since 1850* (Aldershot, 1988). Contains many useful articles.

[79]   A.D. Chandler, *Scale and Scope: the dynamics of industrial capitalism* (Cambridge, MA, 1990).

[80]   D.E.H. Edgerton and S.M. Horrocks, 'British Industrial Research and Development before 1945', *Econ. Hist. Rev.* 47 (1994). The most detailed study of the subject, containing new data. Supplements [73] and refutes [76]. Has extensive bibliography.

[81]   D.E.H. Edgerton, 'British Industrial R&D. 1900–1970', *Journal of Europecn Economic History* 23 (1994). Largely a critique of the tendency to ignore industry in treatments of R&D, the use of misleading statistical measures, and exaggerated nationalism.

[82]   Zvi Griliches, 'Patent Statistics as Economic Indicators: a survey', *Journal of Economic Literature* 28 (1990).

[83]   Walter Vincenti, 'Engineering Knowledge, Type of Design and level of Hierarchy: further thoughts about *What Engineers Know*', in P. Krces and M. Bakker (eds.), *Technological Development and Science in the Industrial Age* (Dordrecht, 1992).

Science, technology and the state

[84]   P.J. Gummett, *Scientists in Whitehall* (Manchester, 1980). Despite the title concerned almost exclusively with civil science. The best general source for government's civil science policy since 1945. Contains extensive bibliography.

[85]   Leslie Hannah, *Engineers, Managers and Politicians: the first fifteen years of nationalised electricity supply in Britain* (1982).

[86]   Fred Steward and David Wield, 'Science, Planning and the State', in G. McLennan *et al.*, *State and Society in Contemporary Britain* (Cambridge, 1984).

[87]   Peter Alter, *The Reluctant Patron: science and the state in Britain* (Oxford, 1987). The best general coverage of government's civil science policy between 1850 and 1920. Despite the title barely mentions the military. Contains an extensive bibliography. Draws especially on the pioneering work of Roy Macleod and his students on the prehistory of British science policy.

[88]   Daniel Headrick, *The Tentacles of Progress. technology transfer in the Age of Imperialism 1850–1940* (New York, 1988). Pioneering study of the diffusion of technologies to colorial territories, especially British ones.

[89]   Roy Sherwood, *Superpower Britain* (Cambridge, 1989). Argues that Britain was ahead of the Americans and Russians in the 1940s and 1950s in selected high technologies, and that this lead was thrown away by incompetent politicians and classically trained civil servants. An excellent statement of the right-wing techno-nationalist view. See also [13]. For analyses of this point of view see [20].

[90]   R. Coopey, R. S. Fielding and N. Tiratsoo (eds.), *The Wilson Governments, 1964–1970* (London, 1993). See in particular the articles by Coopey and Horner.

[91]   D.E.H. Edgerton, 'The "White Heat" Revisited: the British government and technology in the 1960s', *Twentieth Century British History* 7 (1996).

Military science and technology

[92] M.M. Gowing, *Britain and Atomic Energy, 1939-1945* (London, 1964).

[93] R.C. Trebilcock, ' "Spin-off" in British Economic History: armaments and industry, 1760–1914', *Econ. Hist. Rev.*, 22 (1969).

[94] M.M. Gowing, *Independence and Deterrents: Britain and Atomic Energy 1945–1952*, vol. I: *Policy Making*, vol. II: *Policy Execution* (London, 1974) is the official history of the British bomb project and the most detailed study of British warlike technology there is.

[95] J.M. Winter (ed.), *War and Economic Development: essays in memory of David Joslin* (Cambridge, 1975). See in particular the papers by MacLeod and Andrews and by Coleman.

[96] Mary Kaldor, *The Baroque Arsenal* (London, 1982). Argues that the conservative military linked to radical capitalist technology produced baroque weapons.

[97] William H. McNeill, *The Pursuit of Power: technology, armed force and society since AD 1000* (Oxford, 1983). Contains the best general treatment of the British naval industrial complex up to 1914.

[98] David Edgerton and P.J. Gummett, 'Science, Technology, Economics and War in the Twentieth Century', in G. Jordan (ed.), *A Guide to the Sources of British Military History* (New York, 1988). A bibliography.

[99] R.F. Pocock, *The early British Radio Industry*, (Manchester, 1988).

[100] Jon Sumida, *In Defence of Naval Supremacy: finance, technology and British naval policy, 1889–1914* (London, 1989).

[101] David Edgerton, 'Liberal Militarism and the British State', *New Left Review*, No. 185 (1991). Argues that Britain had a particularly technological strategy through the twentieth century, and a strong state apparatus for innovation and procurement in weapons. See also [20] [102][104].

[102] D.E.H. Edgerton, 'Whatever happened to the British Warfare State? The Ministry of Supply, 1945–1951', in Helen Mercer *et al.*, (eds.), *The Labour Government 1945–51 and Private Industry: the experience of 1945–1951* (Edinburgh, 1992). Argues that the Ministry of Supply, and not the Board of Trade, was the key techno-industry ministry under the Labour Government. Also deals with R&D.

[103] R.M. MacLeod, 'The Chemists go to War: the mobilisation of civilian chemists and the British war effort, 1914–18', *Annals of Science* 50 (1993). See the footnotes for other work on science in the Great War, including that by MacLeod himself.

[104] D.E.H. Edgerton, 'Public Ownership and the British Arms Industry, 1920–1950', in Robert Millward and John Singleton (eds.), *The Political Economy of Public Ownership* (Cambridge, 1995).

[105] D.E.H. Edgerton, 'British Scientific Intellectuals and the relations of Science, Technology and War', in Paul Forman and José-Manuel Sanchez Ron (eds.), *National Military Establishments and the Advancement of Science* (Dordrecht, 1996). Details the misleading account given by scientists and the effects this had had on historiography.

Civil science, technology and the state

[106] John Jewkes, *Government and High Technology* (London, 1972). A vigorous pamphlet denouncing the usual arguments for the support by government of 'high' technology. It is not concerned with the military. See also [110][111][118].

[107] L.F. Haber, 'Government Intervention at the Frontiers of Science: British dyestuffs and synthetic organic chemistry, 1914–1939', *Minerva* 11 (1973).

[108] Sir Ieuan Maddock, 'Science, Technology, and Industry', *Proceedings of the Royal Society London*, Pt A, 345 (1975).

[109] N.K. Gardner, 'The Economics of Launching Aid', in A. Whiting (ed.), *The Economics of Industrial Subsidies* (London, 1976).

[110] P.D. Henderson, 'Two British Errors: their probable size and some possible lessons', *Oxford Economic Papers* 29 (1977). The errors are Concorde and the Advanced Gas-cooled Reactor. Excellent example of cost–benefit analysis.

[111] Duncan Burn, *Nuclear Power and the Energy Crisis: politics and the atomic industry* (London, 1978). A scathing study of the British AGR programme, and of British nuclear policy more generally. Attacked the monopoly over nuclear R&D by the AEA, and its poor nuclear technology. Essential reading for anyone who believes that British scientists have been inarticulate, have not had political influence, or have lived in a public world hostile to science and technology.

[112] Russell Moseley, 'The Origins and Early Years of the National Physical Laboratory: a chapter in the prehistory of British Science Policy', *Minerva* 16 (1978).

[113] Russell Moseley, 'Government Science and the Royal Society: the control of the National Physical Laboratory in the interwar years', *Notes and Records of the Royal Society of London* 35 (1980).

[114] Ian Varcoe, 'Co-operative Research Associations in British Industry, 1918–34', *Minerva* 19 (1981).

[115] S.T. Keith, 'Invention, Patents and Commercial Development from Governmentally Financed Research in Great Britain: the origins of the National Research Development Corporation', *Minerva* 19 (1981).

[116] Keith Hayward, *The British Aircraft Industry* (Manchester, 1989). Concentrates on the civil industry as most studies of the subject do. For an alternative view see [20].

[117] Anthony Stranges, 'From Birmingham to Billingham: high-pressure coal hydrogenation in Great Britain', *Technology and Culture* 26 (1985).

[118] P.D. Henderson, *Innocence and Design* (London, 1986). The 1985 Reith Lectures.

[119] P. Palladino, 'The Political Economy of Applied Science: plant breeding research in Great Britain, 1910–1940', *Minerva* 28 (1990).

Comparative

[120] E.H. Lorenz, 'The Labour Process in British and French ship-building from 1880 to 1930', *Journal of European Economic History* 13 (1984).

[121] S.N. Broadberry and N.F.R. Crafts, 'Explaining Anglo-American Productivity Differences in the mid-twentieth century', *Oxford Bulletin of Economics and Statistics* 52 (1990).

[122] S.N. Broadberry and R. Fremdling, 'Comparative Productivity in British and German Industry 1907–37', *Oxford Bulletin of Economics and Statistics* 52 (1990).

[123] N.F.R. Crafts, 'Economic Growth', in N.F.R. Crafts and Nicholas Woodward, (eds.), *The British Economy since 1945* (Oxford, 1991).

[124] Sue Bowden and Avner Offer, 'Household Appliances and the use of time: the United States and Britain since the 1920s', *Econ. Hist. Rev.* 47 (1994).

[125] P. Lundgreen, 'Engineering Education in Europe and the USA, 1750-1930: the rise to dominance of school culture and the engineering professions', *Annals of Science* 47 (1990). The best comparative study.

[126] R. Fox and A. Guagnini (eds.), *Education, Technology and Industrial Performance in Europe, 1850-1939* (Cambridge, 1993). This book contains studies of individual countries, none of which is comparative. See in particular König on Germany and Guagnini on Britain.

[127] B.R. Williams, *Investment, Technology and Growth* (London, 1967). Noted the lack of positive correlation between total R&D and as a proportion of GNP and economic growth. Also noted that this might be due to the inclusion of defence R&D, but did not test this hypothesis.

[128] M.J. Peck, 'Science and Technology', in Richard E. Caves, *Britain's Economic Prospects* (London, 1968). Argues that Britain was overcommitted to science and aerospace R&D.

[129] OECD, *Gaps in Technology: analytical report* (Paris, 1970).

[130] R.C.O. Matthews, 'The Contribution of Science and Technology to Economic Development', in B.R. Williams (ed.), *Science and Technology in Economic Growth* (London, 1973). A useful critical account, noting the lack of positive correlation between civil R&D and growth.

[131] Keith Norris and John Vaizey, *The Economics of Research and Technology* (London, 1973).

[132] C. Freeman, 'Technical Innovation and British Trade Performance', in F.T Blackaby (ed.), *De-Industrialisation* (London, 1978). An extremely influential article, the basis of most of the arguments that imply that British industry underspent on useful R&D in the 1960s and before, because of the high proportion of total industrial R&D devoted to aerospace and defence. Criticised in [135].

[133] Charles Carter (ed.), *Industrial Policy and Innovation* (London, 1981). See especially the paper by Pavitt (88–115) and the comment by Henderson (170–8).

[134] J. Faberberg, 'A Technology Gap Approach to why Growth Rates Differ', *Research Policy* 16 (1987) shows that R&D and patents correlate positively with GDP per capita, and negatively with rates of growth. Misleadingly takes the 'technology gap' to be given by differences in GDP per capita.

[135] David Edgerton, 'Research, Development and Competitiveness', in K. Hughes (ed.), *The Future of UK Industrial Competitiveness and the role of Industrial Policy* (London, 1994). A study of British industrially-funded R&D since 1945, challenging the dominant implication that British industry funded less R&D than that of Germany and Japan in the 1950s and early 1960s.

[136] John Cantwell, 'Historical Trends in International Patterns of Technological Innovation', in James Foreman-Peck (ed.), *New Perspectives in the Late Victorian Economy: essays in quantitative economic history 1860–1914* (Cambridge, 1991).

[137] John Cantwell and Pilar Barrera, 'The Rise of Corporate R&D and the Technological Performance of the largest European Firms from the Interwar years onwards', *Research Policy* (forthcoming).

Additional references

[138] Keith Vernon, 'Science and Technology', in Stephen Constantine, Maurice Kirby and Mary Rose (eds.), *The First World War in British History* (London, 1995). The most complete and up-to-date treatment of British science and technology during and around the Great War. Contains an extensive bibliography.

[139] S.N. Broadberry and K. Wagner, 'Human Capital and Productivity in Manufacturing during the twentieth century: Britain, Germany and the United States', in B. van Ark and N.F.R. Crafts (eds.), *Quantitative Aspects of Postwar European Growth* (Cambridge, 1995). Contains important comparative data on apprenticeship, management education, and R&D. Contains an extensive bibliography.

[140] Paolo Palladino, 'Science, Technology and the Economy: plant breeding in Great Britain, 1920–1970', *Econ. Hist. Rev.* 48 (1995). A study which combines a discussion of the role of science in innovation with an analysis of diffusion and economic impact. Contains an extensive bibliography.

Index

See also the Glossary and the Bibliography for further information. This index covers neither.

New Studies in Economic and Social History

Previously published as

Studies in Economic and Social History

Titles in the series available from the Macmillan Press Limited

11. P. K. O'Brien
   The economic effects of the American civil war

12. S. B. Saul
   The myth of the Great Depression, 1873–1896: second edition

13. P. L. Payne
   British entrepreneurship in the nineteenth century

14. G. C. Peden
   Keynes, the treasury and British economic policy

15. M. E. Rose
   The relief of poverty, 1834–1914

16. J. Thirsk
   England's agricultural regions and agrarian history, 1500–1750

17. J. R. Ward
   Poverty and progress in the Caribbean, 1800–1960

Economic History Society

The Economic History Society of Great Britain, which numbers around 3,000 members, publishes the *Economic History Review* four times a year (free to members) and holds an annual conference.

Enquiries about membership should be addressed to

The Assistant Secretary
Economic History Society
PO Box 70
Kingswood
Bristol
BS15 5TB

Full-time students may join at special rates.